NOT THE
RIGHTEOUS!

NOT THE RIGHTEOUS!

ADAPTED FROM PACIFIC GARDEN MISSION'S
RADIO SERIES, "UNSHACKLED!"

Jack Odell

THE PACIFIC GARDEN MISSION
Chicago 5, Illinois

To Ben Engstrom, of Pacific Garden Mission

Ben will refuse the dedication for himself,
gently chuckle, and give it over to Christ.

CONTENTS

INTRODUCTION

Not the Righteous is a collection of short stories about people who needed to be made whole. They are true stories sensitively written by a man who himself has been made whole. Jack Odell, the dynamic and well-loved announcer on "Unshackled," himself narrated each story when it was broadcast. He knows the people personally and by the time this book is in print, Jack's own amazing story will have been dramatized on "Unshackled." As the former writer of this series, I often sat in the control room of Studio 5 A at WGN in Chicago and *watched* the Holy Spirit of Jesus Christ "take over" the life of Jack Odell during the closing moments of a broadcast on which Jack played the leading role!

This book is an authentic book because the stories are all true and because the one who wrote them is himself an *authentic!* He sees as few Christians see (new or old!) through the fog of misleading *self*-righteousness! He *sees* Jesus Christ as He is, not things *about* Him! Jack Odell *knows,* from his own experience, that this Jesus Christ came to call *not* the righteous, but sinners to repentance! And he knows *why* this is true.

He also knows, along with the devoted men and women who labor day in and day out at the Pacific Garden Mission on Chicago's Skid Row, that "sinner" is not necessarily one lying in an alley or in need of a shave! Jack Odell and I were both in so-called big-time radio for over fifteen years. We remained well-dressed. We were still working. But we were *not* the righteous!

We were sinners and Jesus Christ called us to repentance!

We have prayerfully and carefully selected for inclusion in

9

this book a wide variety of true stories from the some two hundred and fifty broadcast so far on "Unshackled," in the sincere effort to show by actual cases that "all have sinned" and *all* need the cleansing Touch of the One who alone was sinless!

Jack Odell joins me in calling your attention to the unusual vision shown by our sponsors on "Unshackled," the famous old Skid Row Lighthouse, The Pacific Garden Mission of Chicago. I am sure the Lord's Heart rejoices that Superintendent Harry Saulnier and his executive board of Christian businessmen *care* about the lonely, empty, sin-twisted, neurotic "up and outer" as well as the equally lonely, empty, sin-twisted, neurotic "down and outer" shuffling along Chicago's Skid Row streets and alleys. "Unshackled" is reaching into the lives of all kinds of people and because it carries the simple dynamic of the Cross in every broadcast, all kinds of lives are being changed.

These pungently written true stories were poured from the overflowing heart of my Christian brother, and their authenticity will grip you because Jack understands conversion to Jesus Christ! His own darkness was invaded by the Life of God and now the man who once played gangsters and bartenders because he looked the part, fairly "lights up" Studio 5 A on a Saturday night as the Inner-Light shines through his voice and his radiant face!

This same Light shines through these stories in *Not The Righteous!*

They are stranger and more wonderful than fiction, because God Himself wrote them on human lives. If you are inclined to scoff at Christianity and honestly feel no need of Christ, be open-minded enough to read *Not The Righteous!* and then check your reactions against—*truth*. They are each one true.

And they each contain *The Truth.*

If they do not, then Jesus Christ was confused when He declared: *I am the Way, the Truth and the Life!*

Chicago   EUGENIA PRICE

NOT THE
RIGHTEOUS!

*. . . for I am not come to call the righteous,
but sinners to repentance.*

MATTHEW 9:13

Leonard Pollari

. . . who found Living Water

EVERY SCHOOL HAS ITS "BAD BOY." HE'S HELD RESPONSIBLE for sudden increases in cigarette smoking and hooky-playing. When a vulgar new word appears on the play-ground, he starts it.

Leonard Pollari was the "bad boy." He learned to smoke at seven and had a taste for whiskey at twelve. When he was twenty-three, he stood before an Army Psychiatric Board. Discharged "without honor" at twenty-five, he be-came a jobless game poacher and then a fugitive derelict on Chicago's Skid Row. But at thirty-two he became the thing that makes his story worth telling.

Leonard's story begins in Maple, Wisconsin—popula-tion 160. Farming is poor in the iron mining country, but Finnish immigrants have settled there in solid communi-ties. When you see a cloud of steam drifting up among the pines, you can look for a log-walled Sauna, a Finnish steam bath. And Finnish is the second language of the country-side.

It was Leonard Pollari's first language. English came later, and even today he speaks with a little swing.

Leonard was a blonde, curly-haired little black sheep.

13

His mother made that clear to him the first time she found him smoking. Her own serious emotional problems spilled over on Leonard.

"You are a sinful boy!"

Leonard was puzzled.

"What does 'sinful' mean, Mom?"

"It means you are black in the sight of God. You are bad. You please the devil and not God!"

This word "God" he knew, so he used it—blasphemously. The effect on his mother was frightening.

"Don't use the name of God in vain. What did I do to deserve such a boy?" She was near hysteria. "Does God punish me?"

"No, Mommie. No!"

"You curse and you smoke. You will rot like a bad apple in a barrel!"

Leonard was terrified by the outburst. But he kept on smoking in secret, and his vocabulary grew in fluency and profanity.

His mother's emotional condition worsened. In time she was committed to a mental hospital, and when Leonard was twelve, he was farmed out to a neighbor. This man introduced the boy to his first drink of whiskey.

"Leonard, you are—how old?"

"I'm twelve." He snapped the word as though it were twenty.

"So?" The man laughed. "Then you're old enough to drink liquor."

This was a new idea. Leonard was awed at the new challenge to his manhood. The man poured out a stiff jolt of whiskey.

"Here, Lenny. Drink it down."

"All of it?"

"Yeah, like a man. All of it."

Lenny held his breath and drank, bottoms up. And though he gagged, the quick effect on his brain opened a new door of experience. By the time Leonard reached the eighth grade, more on seniority than scholarship, he was a teen-age toper. He traveled the length of Douglas County to crash any celebration where liquor was served, staying until the last bottle was empty.

When the grade school tired of the boy, he graduated into the aimless life of an odd-job man. But for Pearl Harbor he might have remained there.

Conscription is a disaster to some men. But military service gives to others the only purpose and order they've ever known. This was so with Pollari. In the Medical Corps he felt wanted and useful. He became more cheerful and outgoing, and soon earned new responsibilities.

Too much responsibility. Pollari was sent to convoy hospital patients on a transfer by rail, and failed. He got drunk, deserted his patients, and disappeared.

Discipline was limited to company punishment, and Leonard was given another chance. But disgrace made him miserable, and twice more he went AWOL.

He faced the Psychiatric Board three times, each appearance resulting in more drastic punishment. One incident from those hearings tells a great deal. He was trying to be so honest with the board that one member accused him of making fun. At last one doctor asked an oddly penetrating question.

"Pollari, what would you do if I handed you a pint of whiskey right now?"

The answer was simple, revealing, and pitiful.

"Sir, I'd drink half of it—and save the other half for tomorrow morning."

It was the truth, in spite of unbearable shame and a desperate desire to please his commanding officer.

In 1945 Leonard Pollari found himself a civilian, holding one of those ambiguous "blue" discharges. Back in
Wisconsin he drank away the days from one unemployment check to the next.

His gift for trouble stayed with him, and within two
years the game warden wanted him for shooting deer out
of season. This called for a move, so Leonard ran out for
Chicago.

The lights of the Skid Row honkeytonks were Leonard's
Christmas tree in 1947. There on the street he teamed up
with another boy as lost and lonely and self-hating as himself. His buddy's name was George Gedney. Together they
bummed in and out of the saloons, looking for fun they
never found and feeling mutually sorry for themselves.

George had been on the street longer and was first to
strike rock-bottom. He began talking gloomily of suicide.
But Leonard was still looking for something unknown and
unattainable, a glorious adventure that never happened.

That was a cold winter. At the end of weeks of drinking, Leonard's shaky nerves and weakened body needed
warmth and shelter. The door of the Pacific Garden
Mission was open, so he stumbled in.

During that night's meeting, two speakers penetrated
Pollari's awareness, and both for the same reason. "They
smiled so good."

One was a Jew with a glowing face who spoke joyously
about Jesus Christ. The other was a sailor. He talked the
same way and with the same smile.

The sailor found Leonard some food and got him a free
bed in the servicemen's dormitory at the Mission. Sleep-
ing there in an army bunk, Pollari felt almost the same
sense of "belonging" he'd known in the old Medical Corps
squadroom.

When his sailor friend moved on, Leonard went back to

the street. He was afraid someone might "tackle him about religion."

He got a job, built up a nest egg, and then hit the bottle again harder than ever.

In March of 1948, sick and aching, half blind from a blood-clot on an optic nerve, he shuffled into a Harrison Street beanery to spend his last quarter on food. He was eating carefully, hoping the food would stay down, when someone slid onto the next stool and called him by name.

It was his old drinking buddy, George Gedney. Even with a bad eye, Leonard could see that George was *changed.* The man who had so recently talked of suicide was decently dressed. Most amazing, he was smiling. Gloomy George Gedney actually looked happy!

Leonard stared.

"What happened to you, George?"

"What do you mean?" George was grinning.

"You look good. You *smile* so good."

That made George Gedney laugh aloud.

"You mean, I really *look* different?"

Leonard nodded his admiration.

"And I've only been a Christian three weeks. Lenny, this is part of the plan, running into you like this!"

"What plan?" Leonard was lost.

"God's plan, of course. Let's go back to PG together. You've got to have this thing, too, old buddy. You look like you really need it!"

"PG? What's that?"

"Pacific Garden Mission. Wait'll we get there and. . . ."

"I've been there," Leonard broke in. "Hey, you mean you've got religion?"

George laughed again.

"I've got better than that, Leonard. I've got Jesus Christ . . . or maybe it's the other way around. Remember how I used to talk about dying? Well, I'm really *livin'* now, Len. And so is Jesus Christ."

Leonard let George lead him around the corner and down the street to the Pacific Garden Mission. Sick and confused, he knew one thing for certain. Gloomy, miserable George Gedney was a changed man, and Leonard wanted desperately to be changed, too.

He let George take him to the Mission prayer room where they knelt together; and so far as Leonard saw in the light he had, he accepted Christ.

Leonard Pollari stayed at the Mission for a month, building up his weakened body. When he left to live and work outside, he was a man physically, but still an infant spiritually. Away from Christian fellowship he let his attention wander from Christ to self; and he slipped, badly.

He went back to the Mission for help, knowing Who offered strength and healing and forgiveness. This time he stayed a year.

When at last he went out on his own, he again found it hard to keep from stumbling. But now there was a tremendous difference. Tempting as they were, the attractions of the world left him ashamed and unhappy. He had seen the meaning of the Cross, and it left no room for self-pity. He slipped and fell and got up again repeatedly over a two-year period before he finally saw the face of his enemy—and recognized self.

Pride in pocket, he took his problem to Harry Saulnier, superintendent of the Pacific Garden Mission. Leonard stated it with the same honesty he had once brought to the Army Psychiatric Board.

"Why can't I live in the world and not drink? Why do I fail?"

And Harry Saulnier, who sees more alcoholics in a week

than most people do in a lifetime, offered a gentle suggestion.

"Maybe you've been interested *only* in what Christ can do for Leonard Pollari. You see, Leonard, that's reason enough for a man to turn to Him in the *beginning*. But it's not good enough to *grow* on. A baby loves its mother because she means comfort and protection. But as the years go by, the growing child loves his mother for *herself alone*. When he's grown up, he wants to serve instead of to be served. Maybe it's *you* instead of Christ in the center of the picture. Maybe you need to study God's Word instead of yourself. If you want to try it, Leonard, we need you here. . . ."

"You—need me?" Leonard glowed.

"We do. Stay on here and help us. You'll have time to think and study things out."

Leonard took that offer, and began to make an interesting discovery. He puts it this way.

"Mr. Saulnier was right. I'd been studying *me* instead of God's Word. I thought I surrendered to Christ, but all I really gave him was my drinking problem. I tried to give Him the *bottle* and hold onto my right to myself. Now I've turned over *me,* and Christ can have the center of my life. *He* doesn't need to drink—so neither do I."

Now Leonard Pollari speaks confidently for Christ and the Pacific Garden Mission throughout the Middle West. He testifies and his victorious life shows that he will never thirst again because there is, ". . . in him a well of water springing up into everlasting life."

Dan Kearney

. . . an unearned miracle

THEY SAY THE AGE OF MIRACLES IS PAST.

No one stops us on the street to say, "Once I was blind, now I see." No one says, "Yesterday I was a leper; today I'm clean." When a man picks up a bed, he heads for a moving van.

And so, "no miracles," they say.

Dan Kearney is walking proof of miracle, but no crowds follow him. The cleansed don't attract attention. I wonder if someone in Galilee, unknowing, touched a cleansed leper on the arm and said, "Too bad the age of miracles is past. Now, when Moses was alive. . . ."

Dan Kearney is full of contradictions. He walks with the light step of a dancer, but hasn't danced in years. He speaks with the lilt of County Kerry, though he was born in Chicago. His mind is quicker than most, yet he spent three years in a state hospital for the insane. This model of neat-appearing respectability lived for years in gandy camps and hobo jungles.

Dan was born in Chicago in 1900. His father was swept overboard from a lake boat, and the widow suffered from what her neighbors called, "The curse of the dirty drink."

So when Dan was only two, he and his brother John were packed off to Ireland to live with their grandmother.

Kerry is known for beauty. The tallest peaks rise in that corner of Ireland, within sight of Killarney's lakes and the wild seacoast. But without love, beauty doesn't mean much.

It was neither love nor beauty, but the frustrating knowledge of being unwanted that set little Dan Kearney at the age of seven literally to banging his head against a stone wall. And when he bellowed in pain, his grandmother poured out abuse.

"Why don't ye shut yer mouth? 'Tis bad enough that I have to feed you, without I should listen to yer iverlastin' bawlin'."

Out of Danny's sobbing rose a question that had been troubling him.

"Why don't I have a daddy, like Dennis down the street?"

"Because he's washin' around at the bottom of Lake Michigan, by that county of Chicago! He was always a thirsty one. Maybe now he's got his fill."

The boy considered this tender news while she railed on.

"Mind ye don't grow up to be like him, always causin' trouble. Faith, an' yer marked already!"

"Marked, Grandmother? How?"

"Marked to be more trouble, even to God, than ye are good to Him."

So, Dan *was* marked—by rejection.

When he was fourteen, his schoolmaster made it even clearer. He waggled a bony finger in Dan's face.

"Mark my word, Dan Kearney, ye're a bad one. If ye leave off goin' to church and don't mind yer catechism, God will slap ye around until ye're a broken man."

Not long after that episode the grandmother died. Dan and his older brother wandered to Dublin, arriving just in time for the Sinn Fein rebellion of Easter, 1916.

The footloose boys were in the thick of it. Dan served as a messenger between the little groups of rebels, but the rebellion quickly died and left him at loose ends.

The two lads made a precarious living on the Dublin streets. Dan had a talent for entertaining, and his songs and dances brought a few coins along O'Connell Street. By the year 1925 he was a real expert at Gaelic folk-dancing. Meanwhile, John joined the army of the new Irish Free State. Dan never saw him again. Armed with the technicality of American citizenship, he sailed for New York.

Booking agents had little need for Irish dancers. Dan made an uncertain living in Irish dance halls, becoming well known in Irish-American circles in New York and Chicago. There wasn't much money, but always plenty to drink.

When Dan acquired a wife and started rearing a family, he took a full-time job as a bus driver. In less than a year he was fired for drinking. The night it happened, as he gloomed over his tough luck, Dan realized he'd passed over the line that separates the social drinker from the alcoholic.

He knew it, but like many another man, he followed the contradictory pattern of drinking harder to avoid facing reality. Money troubles led to worry, worry led to drinking, and drinking took what money was left.

One night, when Dan came home reeling, Kate asked the classic "why?" He gave her the truth in four slurred but accurate words.

"Because I'm an alcoholic."

"Dan, you're not. You *couldn't* be an alcoholic!"

"Katy, don't make me laugh."

"No, Dan. You don't have to get drunk. If you'll just use your will power and go to church and do like you should, you can take a drop now and then like anyone else!"

"That's very funny, Kate. But I'm *not* laughin'."

The breaking point came on little Danny's third birthday. Dan Kearney was drunker than usual. While the baby wailed and Kate screamed, Dan turned over furniture and flung whatever came to hand. He drove his terrified wife and child from the house and then drank himself into a stupor.

Kate found refuge with a friend, and this started a train of events that put Dan in a state hospital. His wife was ready to follow any advice that came her way. The friend had a plan.

"Send him away and get him fixed up."

"Fixed up?" asked Kate. This was a new idea.

"That's right. They've got a state institution at Kankakee that's a positive cure for alcoholics."

"For—alcoholics? Are you sure?"

"Yes indeed, I'm sure. A lawyer friend of mine fixed up the papers. You sign right here and Dan will be taken care of."

Kate hesitated, then took the pen and signed her husband into a state hospital for the *insane*.

Time dried the alcohol out of Dan's body, but every day of confinement added to his bitterness. Sane though he was, release was almost impossible without his wife's consent.

Kate paid him only one visit. The doctor warned Dan his only hope of freedom lay in persuading her he was sane. Kearney promised his best behavior, but at sight of her his rage boiled over.

"I oughta kill you, Katy," he growled. "I wish I really *was* crazy. Then maybe I could do it!"

"Dan," she said, "I didn't know what kind of place this was. I thought it was a place where they cured alcoholics!"

"What? Are you gonna *lie* on top of everything else?"

"Dan, honest . . . !"

"Get out of here!" Dan was shouting. "I'd rather stay here and rot the rest of my life than to look at the face of a lyin' woman like you! Get out!"

That scuttled his freedom and his marriage. Kate filed for divorce, and Dan lacked the ability to contest it. It was two more years before a very small door of hope opened.

A senior member of the hospital staff had become seriously ill. His convalescence required a full-time attendant. Nurses were in short supply and Dan was given the job. With the assignment his doctor offered some good advice.

"Kearney, if you behave like a sane person on this job, I think I can swing your release. It won't be easy. You're dealing with a difficult man."

Three months later Dan walked out of Kankakee a free man.

He was free of the asylum, but not free from Dan Kearney. And Dan Kearney was despised and rejected, alone in the world. Two weeks of brooding in saloons brought him back to Kankakee. The diagnosis was acute alcoholism.

This time an Alcoholics Anonymous group arranged his release. They tried to help him, but Dan couldn't stay on the program and wouldn't stay put. He ducked out of Chicago, hiding in hobo jungles along the railroad tracks.

This was his toughest time. Dan descended from cheap whiskey to the brain-rotting imitation muscatel of the winoes; then to canned heat squeezed through a rag or a chunk of bread. When he could get dope, he used it. Anything to dull his agony of fear and bitterness.

In 1948 he drifted back to Chicago. Penniless and sick, he was literally unable to speak more than a few words without weeping or cursing. On September twenty-third he reached bottom.

Clinging to a lamp post across the street from the Pacific Garden Mission, he tried to muster nerve enough to throw himself under the wheels of a "Green Hornet" streetcar. To this day Dan has no clear memory of blundering through traffic to the Mission door nor of talking to the man who held it open for him, but his mumblings told the story.

He had come because the Mission sign read, "Jesus Saves."

Dan became defiant, though, when Harry Saulnier, the Mission superintendent, tried to talk to him about Jesus.

"I know all about Jesus," he shouted.

"You do?"

"Sure." Dan coughed, then went on. "I learned all about Him when I was a boy. He's the second person in the Holy and Undivided Trinity."

Harry Saulnier had a lot to tell Dan about Jesus, but first came a dinner, shower, and clean clothes. Then he massaged Dan's aching feet and the legs with their splotchy wine-sores.

Twenty centuries ago Peter said, *"Thou shalt never wash my feet."*

In 1948 Dan Kearney said, "Why should you rub my feet? I'm no good."

Harry told him, "None of us is any good till we've been cleaned up by Jesus Christ."

Dan was puzzled.

"Hey, what religion is there here at this place?"

"Just—Christianity, Dan. This is a personal thing between Jesus Christ and you."

"Jesus Christ—and me? I don't get the connection."

But before that night was over, Dan Kearney did get the connection as he listened to Harry Saulnier speaking from the platform of the Pacific Garden Mission.

He heard Harry read from the Bible, *"There is one God, and one mediator between God and men, the man, Christ Jesus."*

When the service ended, he knelt in the old prayer room and received Jesus Christ as his personal Saviour.

That's the traditional ending for conversion stories, but Dan still had troubles ahead.

His next bender ended with the only kidnaping in the Mission's history. Harry Saulnier hauled Dan bodily out of a saloon. Hardly standard evangelistic procedure, but Harry Saulnier is a bold man in the Lord.

Next day, Dan was grateful, repentant, and puzzled. He took his questions to Saulnier.

"Look, you're makin' this too easy. I oughta have to— do something to earn forgiveness."

"Jesus earned our forgiveness, Dan, when He gave Himself in our stead on the Cross. We can only take it. It's a gift."

There is a Christian farm for alcoholics at Keswick Grove, New Jersey. Its slogan is, "Where men are *trans*formed, not *re*formed." The Mission sent Dan to Keswick.

There he grew physically strong, but he was weak in faith. He talked it over with one of his new friends, a big, cheerful Pole named Lolly Papete.

"Lolly, I can't seem to get at Christ personally! It makes me sore and then I want a drink."

"Maybe you block Him with doubt."

"That's it. I doubt Him. Look, how do I know I'm gonna be with Jesus when I die? You *know* I'm gonna die with some kind of sins in my life!"

"Yah, Dan, but our line to Jesus is straight. Because I believe in Him, I am one with the Father. The Bible says, ". . . whosoever believeth in him should not perish, but have everlasting life."

"I know, Lolly, but . . ." —Dan was pacing back and forth in his excitement. ". . . but I'd be scared to die right now without a last chance to clear myself with God. Wouldn't you? Wouldn't you be scared to drop dead right now?"

"Scared of God?" Lolly smiled gently. "Why Dan, 'The Lord is my shepherd,' and even though I walk through the valley of the shadow of death, I shall fear no evil."

That night Dan prayed for a sign from God to help his unbelief. But he passed the days that followed in an agony of doubt.

Then Lolly Papete collapsed in the dining hall and was carried unconscious to the hospital.

As Dan prayed in his room, someone brought word that his Polish friend had died without regaining consciousness. Dan knew Lolly hadn't had time to, "clear himself with God."

Deeply troubled, he picked up his Bible.

"Somewhere in the Book, God can speak right straight out to me, Dan Kearney."

He leafed quickly through the pages. Something caught his eye at the end of the fourth chapter of First Thessalonians. For the first time he read, *"For if we believe that Jesus died and rose again, even so them also which sleep in Jesus will God bring with him. . . . For the Lord himself shall descend from heaven with a shout, with the voice of the archangel, and with the trump of God: and the dead in Christ shall rise first. Then we which are alive and remain shall be caught up together with them in the clouds, to meet the Lord in the air: and so shall we ever be with the Lord. Wherefore comfort one another with these words."*

Dan slowly put the Bible back on the table and sank to his knees.

"I'm through fighting You, Lord. You spoke right to me, Dan Kearney, and I believe You!"

And Dan took, as a gift, that which is free and cannot be earned.

On a recent summer evening, I talked with Dan Kearney on a busy street corner. He spoke of his Bible studies and his hopes for a Christian rehabilitation farm near Chicago. Though thousands of people passed, no one looked twice at this neat little man whose life is proof of miracle.

I wondered how many of those tense-faced people were walking in silent desperation with the painful belief that nothing but a miracle could ease their troubles, and laughing bitterly at themselves because, "the age of miracles is past."

At last Dan walked off into the crowd; a happy, quietly radiant man. He was heading back to the door over which the burning letters read, "Jesus Saves."

No one followed him.

I remembered that the cleansed lepers showed no scars, and that the healed blind man threw away his staff.

Scotty Lawrence

. . . who played God

"GENTLEMEN, I CAN WRITE A COMPLETE SONG, WORDS AND music, in twenty minutes."

Scott Lawrence was holding court in a gas-lit barroom, surrounded by a thirsty entourage of hangers-on. The oak table was round, but it clearly had a head. That was where Scott Lawrence sat.

Scotty was monarch of New York's song writers and looked the part. He was the prototype of all the vagabond kings and student princes that have ever smiled across the footlights. Also, Scott Lawrence was drunk.

He was drunk, but not out of control. In those days he was never out of control; always self-possessed, and possessed with self. Loss of control lay ahead in the days of, "The king is dead." Tonight the courtiers were shouting, "Long live the king," and Scotty loved it.

He pounded the table for silence.

"I said it, and I mean it, and I can do it. I can write a complete song, words *and* music, in twenty minutes!"

While they laughed and protested he finished his drink.

"And what's more, it'll be a big one. They'll sing it all over the country!"

A rival songwriter stood up to call Scotty's bluff.

"Scotty, you're good, but you're not that good. I say, 'put your money where your mouth is!' "

That brought out the wallets and money. Laughing delightedly, Scotty produced a roll of green backs and peeled it with a moistened thumb.

"Did someone mention ten to one?"

Money began fluttering onto the table, and the bluff was called.

Scott Lawrence lit a fresh cigar, poured himself another drink, and sat down at an empty table with a big gold watch ticking away the time. His only tools were a sharpened pencil, the back of a theater program, and matchless self-assurance.

Twenty minutes later he had a half-chewed cigar, an empty glass, and the manuscript of America's latest hit song. Also, his self-assurance was completely intact.

A song plugger took the manuscript to the piano while Scotty pocketed his winnings. Two minutes later the plugger gave the saloon audience a premier performance of, "I'll Never Be Good Enough."

No one noticed that Scott Lawrence was wearing his heart on his sleeve.

There has always been something especially dramatic about a really good woman's love for a dissolute man. It gives her a tragic luster and turns out the linty pockets of his character.

The name of the girl in this story was Victoria Barnes. Vicky had no illusions about Scott Lawrence. She saw him with clear eyes and heard the clink of his counterfeit character, and still she loved him. And so, of course, she always would.

Scott Lawrence loved Victoria second to none in this world with the exception of Scott Lawrence.

"I'll Never Be Good Enough" grew to hit proportions. Victoria knew, of course, that it was written for her. But she wasn't fooled by the hollow self-pity of the title. She pretended not to notice, and this forced Scotty into the open. Typically, his campaign centered around Scott Lawrence.

Victoria had been running through a group of old songs at her piano. When she stopped playing, Scotty spoke.

"Vicky, why don't you play something new? What about 'I'll Never Be Good Enough'?"

Victoria smiled and said nothing.

"It's written by a very successful reprobate named Scott Lawrence. Ever hear of him?"

"Yes," she said. "I love him."

"Then why. keep me at arm's length? I believe you love me, Vicky, but you're so cold. Why aren't you more like I am? You don't even speak my language, Vic. You're too . . . too good."

She turned to face him. "Scotty, do you honestly want me to change? Do you really want me to come over to your side?"

He couldn't answer that.

"Would you still love me as much—if I changed?"

Still he said nothing.

"Scotty—will you answer me?"

Somehow, he told the truth.

"No, Vic. No, I wouldn't."

Then he grabbed for the self-deception that has launched so many unhappy marriages.

"You can change me, Vicky. Marry me, and you can make me like—like you are. You can change me, Vicky!"

It's a fiction that few women have ever been able to resist. It has the shape of love, the fabric of mercy, and the color of hope. Victoria sat quietly in her own little wilderness, hardly knowing what to pray for.

Fragments of a sentence fluttered in her mind. *"Get thee hence, for it is written. . . ."* She had her answer.

"No, Scotty—I can't. That's what you won't seem to understand. Only—God—can change you."

"Leave Him out of it. That's one thing I *don't* have to put up with!"

"Scotty, listen." She was suddenly close to tears. "God is love—and He wants us together. But He knows you and I can never be happy as long as you're playing God, too. There can't be two Gods in one home, Scotty. It just won't work!"

Scotty's pride had a choice. It could resist or it could bend. And because it wouldn't bend, he rejected the thing he loved.

"You win, Vicky." He stood up. "I can see it won't work. You've made it very clear, my dear. Suddenly I *believe* it won't work."

Even then she still tried.

"We can have a beautiful life, Scotty. But you've got to turn to God. You need Him. God loves you—and so do I."

Scotty was furious.

"He doesn't love me—and I *don't* need Him! I'll still be my own god, Victoria, and I'll prove to you that it works. I don't need anybody—not even you!"

He stormed out. Victoria Barnes, on her knees beside the piano bench, did the only thing that was left to do. She prayed.

During the years that followed, Victoria kept up with Scotty's progress through the theatrical papers. He did well for a long time, touring the country as an arranger and song writer with the top vaudeville acts of the day. The stack of songs with "words and music by Scott Lawrence" grew taller and taller on her piano.

When Scotty thought of Victoria, it was always in terms of his injured pride. If his heart was broken, one fragment pumped self-esteem and the other self-pity. Together they beat for Scott Lawrence.

The self-worshiper faces one great danger. He may eventually get a candid, revealing view of his deity. There's a traditional solution, and Scotty used it. He hid his one man holy of holies behind an alcoholic veil. When that screen dissolved in the light of too many mornings-after, he reinforced it with cocaine.

With the years, Vicky found fewer and fewer Scott Lawrence tunes to add to her collection. Finally, they stopped appearing at all. The king was professionally dead.

As his name dropped out of the theatrical papers, Scotty dropped out of sight below the police deadline in Chicago. There on the old Levee Scotty pounded pianos to pay for the whiskey and dope that held him together.

Through the years Victoria waited and prayed. When Scotty disappeared, she tried to reach out by setting a net of prayer. She asked the rescue missions in New York to pray regularly for Scott Lawrence. They in turn passed the request on to missions all over the country. For ten years Scotty's name was forgotten everywhere—except in mission prayer meetings.

He knew nothing of all this, for a mission was the last place he intended to go. As a member of the sizeable cult of self-worship he needed first to reach a sort of special atheism and lose faith in himself. After that he could look up and discover that God had been waiting all the time.

There's a definite mark in Scott Lawrence's history at the point where he lost faith in his own deity.

On that day, stooped and ragged and shaking, he

shuffled into one of Chicago's biggest department stores
and openly lifted an expensive handbag from one of the
counters. He was purposely attracting as much attention
as possible. A store detective caught him, of course.

While they waited for the wagon, the detective said,
"What's the matter with you bums, anyway? You might
know you'd wind up in the clink."

Then and there Scott Lawrence recanted his faith in
Scott Lawrence.

"That's what I'm hopin' for. Because outside of jail—
I'm hopeless!"

He served six months in the Bridewell prison. Faith in
self was gone, and he'd found no other faith to replace it.
When he came out of jail, he was too much of a wreck to
be accepted even below the deadline. The night came
when, lying on two broken boxes in an alley under a
drenching rain, he thought he'd reached the end.

There in that filth-littered alley, the phantoms in his
brain began talking to him. They used the voice of the
woman he had walked out on years before. Words filtered
back out of the past.

*"We can have a beautiful life, Scotty. But you've got
to turn to God."*

He whimpered softly.

"Scotty, you need Him. God loves you—and so do I."

The man crawled to his feet and stumbled toward the
mouth of the alley, water running in and out of his broken
shoes.

"God loves you, Scotty."

He struggled to move faster, running raggedly toward
the lights of the street.

"Oh, God—I'm losing my mind!"

The doors of the Pacific Garden Mission have never
closed, but at one o'clock on that rainy night the chapel
was quiet. Ma Taylor, wife of the superintendent, was

dimming the lights as Scott Lawrence, tattered and dripping, came stumbling in.

She led him to a bench and sat quietly as he told his story. When he gave his name, she said, "Oh, praise God," and stopped him.

"This is an answer to more prayers than you'll ever know about."

Scotty was puzzled. "Prayers, ma'am?"

"Thousands of prayers. Missions in Chicago and New York and I don't know how many other cities have been praying for Scott Lawrence for ten years!"

"Praying for *me*? Why?"

"Because someone asked for prayer. The request was sent around the New York missions first. Then it was passed along to us."

Tears rose in Scotty's bloodshot eyes. He slowly put the information together as he faltered, "Requests—for prayer —from New York?"

"I don't know who made the request, but. . . ."

"I know." Then, "I'm here—what do I do?"

There was only one real answer, of course. Ma Taylor talked to Scotty about Jesus, and she was led to emphasize "He loves you."

At last she said, "Do you believe Jesus really came out of that tomb and is alive now and willing to save you from yourself, if you'll let Him?"

Bruised and battered, Scotty's ego still resisted.

"Do I believe that?"

"I didn't say 'do you understand it?' I'm asking, 'Do you *believe* that Christ can straighten out your life?' "

"I should, ma'am, because I've been proven wrong. And I've been trying to play God—in my own life."

Ma Taylor smiled as she answered, "That's the best definition of sin I've heard in a long time."

Together they read, *"But as many as received him, to*

*them gave he power to become the sons of God, even to
them that believe on his name."*

And Scotty received Jesus Christ into his life.

But an ego like his doesn't surrender easily. That rainy
night began Scotty's most violent time of conflict. He
shuttled between alternate spells of sobriety and saturation.
The pattern was standard: rebellion, intoxication, and
then remorse and prayer at Pacific Garden Mission. A
sober interlude followed, and then rebellion and the full
cycle again. Mrs. Taylor patiently worked and prayed with
him when others gave up.

During one of the times of remorse she said, "Scotty, do
you feel as though you're still hunting for something—
something you haven't found?"

"I don't know how you knew, but you're right."

"If you feel unsatisfied," Ma Taylor went on, "it's because you don't *belong* to Christ. You need to stop trying
on your own strength and really surrender yourself."

"Surrender?"

"That's the word. You have Jesus Christ, But He doesn't
have *you.*"

He thought that over and Mrs. Taylor went on.

"Tell me, Scotty, what do you keep going back out there
for? What's out there on the street?"

"Nothing, ma'am. There's really nothing out there."

"Then let go of 'nothing' and give yourself all the way
to Him. He loves you, Scotty. And you need Him."

These were Victoria's own words. "He loves you. You
need Him."

This time they penetrated—to stay.

The following morning a very different Scott Lawrence
sat at the Mission piano, working out new melodies that
needed to be heard.

Scotty's talents were free to flow again, but they flowed
for the glory of his new Lord. Within months his gospel

songs were echoing coast to coast, from one mission chapel to another.

Once sure of his new freedom, Scotty followed the trail of an old prayer request back to New York City. He was unable to find Victoria, but while he searched he kept on writing songs and speaking at prayer meetings and revivals.

One of Scotty's new songs was, "Whisper A Prayer." It was introduced in a big New York auditorium. When the music ended, he was called from the audience to the platform.

As he started down the aisle a tall, slender woman rose from a seat near the front and came up the same aisle toward him.

"Scotty—I was afraid to wait until after the service. I'd hate to lose you again!"

Holding hands like children, Victoria went up to the platform with him.

They had five wonderful years of married life and then one day Victoria wrote a long letter to Mrs. Walter G. Taylor at Chicago's Pacific Garden Mission. It began this way:

Yes, Scott has gone home. But during the five years we worked together among underprivileged children here in New York City, my Scotty more than made good. His going was as sweet and quiet as a baby falling asleep.

And the letter ended:

When you feel discouraged there at the Mission and the results seem hopeless, please remember Scott and gain new courage. Whatever you do, with Christ's help, say over and over again, "It can be done, it has been done and will be done again."

> Your happy sister,
> Mrs. Scott Lawrence."

Dick Lane

... who bore the marks

IF ONE NEEDED MATERIAL ON "THE ESSENCE" OF SIN, Dick Lane would be a useful exhibit. It isn't merely that he was a criminal. What other criminals did, he *overdid*. He was cruel for the sake of cruelty itself. Through his career a line of brutality reaches back from Lane to Cain; a bloody streak that could only be washed clean in Blood. His character doesn't make sense in any terms but *sin*. No painful experience in his early life shows why Dick Lane was a deliberately cruel man.

Around the turn of the century, he was one of the best safe blowers in the business. Even the best get caught, and he was well known by the police of a dozen cities. Because he was brilliant and daring as well as cruel, the police reporters often discussed him among themselves. At last he came to the attention of a Chicago newspaper executive. This man decided Dick was worth saving. He made up his mind to offer the safe blower a job and a chance to go straight.

A reporter passed the word to the underworld, and Dick agreed to a meeting. It took place in a cafe. The two men sized each other up for a moment, then the businessman opened the conversation.

"Lane, you just don't look the type. Why don't you change your line from burglary to business?"

Dick Lane sneered.

"Put the money in the safe for some other guy to steal? Do I look stupid?"

"No, and you don't look like a criminal, either."

Lane's eyes glittered. "Looks are very deceiving, mister." His voice purred. "Look at you, for instance. You look like a two-bit pickpocket."

That was Dick Lane. He never missed a chance to be cruel.

"Lane—it doesn't matter what you think I look like. We're here to talk about helping *you*. Don't you want help?"

"Not the kind you want to give me."

The executive tried again.

"Listen, Lane—if you'd make good in one legitimate job, the law would get off your back."

"How do you mean?"

"You're in Chicago on a twenty-four hour time limit. You can be picked up on sight. Now, if you'll go to work in my circulation department, I'll ask the Commissioner to drop that pickup order."

"Sure," Dick laughed, "he'll say 'yes' and the coppers'll pick me up the next day. They're bigger crooks than I am."

"Give it a try, Lane. Give me a chance to help you."

The safe blower pushed back his chair.

"Mister, I don't want your help, and I don't need it. Yours or anyone else's."

That was the interview. During the years that followed, other well-meaning men tried to give Dick a hand, but they all got the same answer.

Like all habitual criminals, Dick Lane was caught and imprisoned repeatedly. In penitentiaries he was known

as a tough "con." The other prisoners hated him because
he hated *them*.

He particularly hated the youngsters and enjoyed bait-
ing young first offenders. When one of them tried to earn
a good conduct parole, Dick set out to spoil his chances. He
knew all the tricks—hiding his victim's tools, stealing his
few possessions, muttering threats, even inflicting bodily
injury when he could get away with it. Sooner or later, this
persecution drove his victim to an outburst of fury. Then
the good conduct record was ruined. Dick spoiled the
efforts of a good many kids to rehabilitate themselves.

It was Lane's contempt for decency that led to the first
crack in his self-assurance.

In Toledo, Ohio, an eighteen-year-old boy was converted to Christ. He read in his Bible a passage from the
twenty-fifth chapter of Matthew:

*Or when saw we thee sick, or in prison, and came unto
thee?*
*And the King shall answer and say unto them, Verily I
say unto you, Inasmuch as ye have done it unto the least
of these my brethren, ye have done it unto me.*

Challenged by the Scripture, the boy went to visit
prisoners in the city jail.

Smiling and friendly, he reached through the bars of a
cell to offer his hand. The prisoner was Dick Lane.

"Beat it."

"Sir, I want to shake your hand."

Lane spat on the floor. "Beat it, kid, or I'll call the
turnkey."

"Don't do that," the boy pleaded. "I've got good news
for you."

"Such as?"

The lad stood close to the bars.

"You can get out of all this!"

Lane looked quickly up and down the corridor. Then he cautioned, "Careful, kid!"

"But I mean it, mister. You can be free. I've just found out about it. It works, too!"

"Yeah?"

"You want to be out of all this, don't you?"

"Jail?"

"Yes, sir. Jail, and your life of crime—and *sin*. All of it!"

For just a moment, crafty Dick Lane had been taken in by his desire for freedom. Now he was suddenly cagey.

"Sin?" Lane breathed the word much too gently.

"Yes, sir. It's sin that's holding you here. Not these bars."

"You mean it, kid?"

"I certainly do. Just as it was sin that nailed Jesus Christ to the Cross. *Our* sin nailed Him there because He wanted to set us free. I've just become a Christian; and I want you to be one too, because I want you to be free."

Lane's voice was silky. "You do?"

"Yes, sir." The boy's eyes were shining. "I'm free because I've put my faith in Jesus Christ—and I want you to be free like I am."

He faltered, then plunged ahead.

"I might have been afraid of someone like you before. But now I'm willing to do like Saint Paul wrote and, 'bear in my body the marks of the Lord Jesus.' Will you let me help you, sir?"

Dick Lane studied the earnest, freckled face for a long moment.

"Kid . . . ?"

"Yes, sir?"

"Do you still want to shake hands with me?"

"Oh, yes sir. I certainly do!"

He gave his hand to the old cracksman.

Lane's shock-cord muscles clamped tight and twisted

savagely. There was a sharp cry and a sickening snap of bone. Dick Lane released his grip and quietly stepped back.

Tears filled the boy's eyes as he looked first at his broken arm and then at the man in the cell.

Lane said, "You had to learn, kid."

The boy's voice was twisted with pain.

"I'd let you break the *other* arm—if it would break the thing that's made you this way."

This was something Dick Lane couldn't endure.

"Get out of my sight! If I could get at you, I'd kill you!"

The boy said, "I guess you've showed me—what Saint Paul really meant."

"What are you talkin' about?"

" 'Henceforth let no man trouble me: for I bear in my body the marks of the Lord Jesus.' "

The boy left quietly, and the safe cracker never saw him again.

But the snapping bone seemed to have snapped something inside Dick Lane. From that time he aged rapidly, and his cold assurance oozed away. The underworld paid well for each job, but he began noticing that his hands shook as he placed his explosive charges of "soup." With his nerves failing, he passed more and more of the tough jobs along to younger men.

The word went out that Dick Lane was cracking up, and within months he was a beaten, frightened has-been in the world of crime. Still he had to keep moving. Policemen refused to let the sun set on Dick Lane in their jurisdiction, and he was nudged from town to town.

Chicago still allowed him twenty-four hours. He took advantage of that allowance to call on the newspaperman whose help he'd once refused.

That man understood the meaning of "the second mile." Dick left the office with the first legitimate job he'd ever held. He had been made a receiving clerk on the old Chicago *Record-Herald*. When he convinced the Chicago police he was actually on a payroll, they lifted the twenty-four hour limit.

By some standards, old Dick was a free man. But this kind of freedom was a bitter thing because he was still shackled—to himself and to *sin*. On the job, he was too busy to think much about himself. His troubles began in the evening. With nothing to do, he walked the streets for hours at a time, always lonely and troubled by old memories. With his toughness gone, he couldn't shake the memories off, and they left him afraid and ashamed. At times he found himself almost running, but he didn't know what it was he was running from.

He wondered if these nights of walking alone were affecting his sanity. The time came when he was desperate for companionship.

That night, as he passed the lighted door of the Pacific Garden Mission, Dick stopped on the pavement to listen to the sound of people singing. As he stood, someone touched his arm.

"Hello. Come on in. You're just in time for the service."

The man was young and tall, with a friendly grin. His smile may have reminded Dick of that other young face in the Toledo jail. Lane hesitated, then nodded and followed him into the Mission.

Once, during the hymns, Dick leaned over and whispered, "You put me in mind of another young fellow I knew once. He was a Christian boy, too. He wanted to help me."

"So do I, sir, if you'll let me."

After the meeting, they talked for a long time about his loneliness and his fears. Dick's new friend spoke of Jesus Christ, who said, ". . . *my peace I give unto you.*"

That night, kneeling at the altar of the old lighthouse,

Dick Lane was led into a new life with Christ. The Mission files describe the transformation that followed in the words, "glorious and amazing." The man whose lifelong hostility had shriveled into cowardice became a courageous and saintly man of God!

Dick found a small furnished room near the Mission. There was plenty of work to fill his free time. Every boy in trouble "put him in mind" of the one whose arm he'd broken, and over the years he helped scores of them.

When a homeless boy needed shelter, the old man was always willing to share his quarters. Some of these young guests were frightened and sick, others tough and defiant. Either way, he worked patiently to lead them to his Lord Jesus. There was always a little left out of his salary to help them.

One of the tough ones was a big, defiant redhead. He figured Dick for an easy mark and cooked up a hard luck story. His mother was dying, he said, and he needed fifteen dollars for a railroad ticket to his home town.

Dick listened and nodded. He was willing to be "a fool for Christ." He knew that if Red was ever to be converted he must first see Christ in Dick. To get the money Red said he needed, they climbed the worn stairs to the old man's room.

Dick opened the door, stepped inside, and touched a match to the gas mantle on the wall.

"Want a cup of coffee, Red? Won't take but a minute."

"Just the fifteen bucks, Mr. Lane."

"Sure, Red." Dick paused. "Got some fresh doughnuts. How about a doughnut?"

"Just the *dough*. Have you got it, or is this a stall so you can read the Bible to me?"

Dick chuckled. "I'd like to read the Bible to you, Red. Nothing I'd like better. But we came here to get your fifteen dollars. Sooo. . . ."

White-haired old Dick Lane turned away, reached behind the clock on the shelf, and took down a tin box. Behind him the boy drew a sharp, nervous breath.

"That where you keep your dough, Lane?"

Dick stood still. His lifetime experience of crime told him what was happening, yet his voice was gentle when he spoke.

"Yeah, Red. What little I've got. Why?"

A pistol shot answered. The old man slumped to the floor. Red reached for the tin box as it clattered against the dresser.

If Red hadn't been caught a few days later, we'd never know the story of those last few minutes. But it all came out in his confession to the police. Even after they typed out the confession and he signed it, Red still had something on his mind.

"You know—the old guy was kinda—funny."

"What do you mean?" the detective asked.

"What he said after he fell, when I grabbed the box."

"Yeah? What was it?"

"He says to me, 'Son, I'd give you more than that if I thought it would help you.' "

The young hoodlum paused, remembering.

"Then he says somethin' else. Maybe it was from the Bible. He was always readin' outa the Bible."

"So what did he say?" The detective was in a hurry.

"I remember it pretty good. It was somethin' like, 'No man can trouble me, for I bear in my body—the marks of the Lord Jesus.' "

The boy paused again.

"And then what, Red?"

"Then he died—real easy."

Dick Ramey

... masterpiece

"STEAMBOAT 'ROUND THE BEND!"

Three quarters of a century ago those were magic words, and barefoot country kids came running to see the big sternwheelers. Dick Ramey was only ten when he lost his heart to the Ohio River and the woodburning packets.

His people were "Kentucky Hoosiers," scratching a poor existence out of a small farm on the Indiana shore. The life was hard, and Dick lived for the day he could be a riverman. A strong boy was needed to help out on the farm, but when he was twelve, in spite of his mother's pleading and his father's bad health, he ran away.

In those days boys went to work early. Dick was big for his age and had no trouble finding a job aboard a steamer. He found the gypsy life to his liking. Lying on the lower deck with the white water foaming close beside him and the green bank sliding past, Dick came close to complete contentment. With a new scene around every bend, it was easy to forget the neglected responsibilities at home.

Restlessness returned when the hawsers were out at a landing. Then he went ashore with the older men and learned new ways to deaden an uneasy conscience. By the time he was fifteen, Dick was a hard drinker and a habitual gambler.

When winter closed the river, he drifted home. But each spring the first distant hoot of a steam whistle pulled him back to the Ohio.

The winter Dick began calling on one of the neighborhood girls his mother had hope she might persuade him to settle down, and as his interest in Mary Ransom grew warmer she opened a full scale campaign to keep him on the land.

"Dick," she began, "when are you gonna marry and settle down?"

"When I want to. *If* I ever want to."

"You been seein' a lot of Mary Ransom lately. You think she's a mighty purty girl, don't you, son?"

"Maybe I do, and maybe I don't. Anyway, it ain't none of your business."

"It is now, son. Mary made it my business. She come to see me last week."

"Yeah?" Dick shuffled restlessly.

"Yes, she did. She wants me to tell you that she'll marry you . . . if you'll settle down to farmin' and quit the river."

"What farm? This one?"

"No, son. One her Pa just deeded to her. Mary and the farm are yours for the askin'."

"And what if I'm not interested?"

"Then I'd say you're a mighty foolish boy."

When the winter broke, the question was still undecided. Dick went back to the river. He knew he wanted Mary. They'd become very close that year. But he wanted his freedom, too. He was a drifter by nature and he wanted to keep on drifting.

All that summer he struggled with his indecision. The problem followed him up and down the Ohio and in and out of dozens of waterfront saloons and gambling houses. When ice in the river sent him home again, the choice was still to be made.

Long before the next spring came around, Dick knew he wanted the girl most of all. Still he tried to work out an impossible compromise. He made one big effort to persuade her.

"Mary, I want you on the river with me."

"What?"

"Sure, we could get a houseboat and. . . ."

"No, Dick!"

"You'd love it out there on the river, Mary—with me. . . ."

"I know I would. It's not the river. It's the life that goes with it—the drinkin' and the gamblin'. I'd lose you in no time."

Dick was loaded with good intentions.

"I'd give all that up, honey. I promise I would."

"No use to promise, Dick. It just wouldn't work."

Dick was a gambler, but Mary was a better one—as women usually are. She staked everything on an ultimatum.

"Dick, it has to be the farm—or nothin'."

It was choose or lose, and Dick Ramey chose.

That spring he couldn't hear the whistles for the wedding bells. Dick made an honest effort to make good as a farmer, but his heart was never really in the dull and tiring routine. When the old restlessness came back, he began slipping off to town on Saturdays. As time went by the weekends lengthened. He often stayed away until Monday or Tuesday.

The neglected farm ran down and the income dwindled. Dick talked Mary into a mortgage and tried to pyramid his cash at the gambling tables. It's a gambler's axiom that frightened money never wins. Dick was no exception. He lost at the tables even faster than he had at farming. In time he piled up a gambling debt he couldn't meet.

The crisis came on his thirtieth birthday. Professional gamblers have unique and terrifying methods of collecting delinquent accounts. They gave him just twenty-four hours to pay up and backed their demand with serious threats.

It was a tight spot, but Dick had a plan. It called for his wife's help, and though she knew it was wrong, Mary at last agreed to use her influence. The problem was persuading Dick's father to mortgage the old family farm for enough to cover the debt. Where Dick might fail, an appeal from Mary was certain to succeed. As he harnessed the team for the drive to his parents' place, he felt his troubles were at an end. When Mary wished him a happy birthday, he laughed and kissed her. Everything was going to be fine, and he had a quart bottle hidden under the wagon seat.

Dick's father was standing near the gate to meet them. As they drew near he raised his hand in greeting. Then, as they waved back, the old man stiffened in sudden agony and fell to the ground. He was unconscious when Dick carried him into the house.

Driving to notify the doctor, Dick tried to steady himself with the bottle. His plans for paying off the gamblers were tottering. The outlook became worse when the doctor completed his examination and gave an opinion.

"I don't believe he can live more than a few days."

Dick's problem overrode his grief.

"Doc—do you s'pose he could—uh, sign a paper in the shape he's in?"

"Sign a paper? Dick, the man's unconscious. He's dying!"

"Yeah, I know, Doc. But won't he . . . ?"

"Regain consciousness?"

"Yeah."

"I doubt it. He'll likely hang on for a few days, but I expect him to remain unconscious."

The doctor drove off. Mary went home alone to care for the stock. When Dick's mother went to bed, he was left alone with his dying father, his bottle, and his problem.

Without the old man's signature there could be no mortgage. But the gambling debt stood. Dick was dealing with ruthless men who demanded a sure thing.

Life insurance is a sure thing, and the elder Ramey had life insurance. But it takes a corpse to make it sure.

The old man's shallow, tired breathing went on and on. Dick listened and drank and watched the clock. He recalled stories of drawn-out illnesses, of dying men who clung to life when hope was gone.

He shuddered at his own imaginings and drank deep from the bottle. The pale corn-likker burned its way down and he stopped shaking. The evil ideas stayed with him.

"One day—two days—three days—a week. What's the difference? He's dead right now, and too stubborn to stop breathing."

Ramey stood slowly and lurched to the bed. He leaned over. The closed eyes and parted blue lips fascinated him. He reached out and placed his hands lightly, experimentally around the dry, scrawny neck. Was his problem really this simple? All he needed was a moment's resolution. The blood pounded in his head. He drew a sharp, spasmodic breath.

The eyes of the dying man fluttered open.

"Dick. . . ."

Ramey pulled his hands away. The faint, whispering voice spoke again.

"God—forgive you, son."

A pause—and again . . .

"God—forgive you!"

The faded eyes closed.

Dick Ramey turned away and tilted the bottle until every drop had run down his throat. Then he slumped back into his chair. The tired breathing went on and on.

The end came quietly a few hours later. Whatever lay on Dick's conscience, his hands were unbloodied. He had an insurance policy and a corpse. The gamblers were willing to wait for their sure thing.

At the funeral, Dick was unable to look into the casket. Nor could he meet his mother's eyes. Neighbors took his haggard look for a sign of mourning, but the thing that gnawed at him was far worse. He lived every hour with the knowledge of how near he had come to murdering his own father.

In the months that followed, familiar surroundings were unbearable. Ramey's restlessness and his drinking increased. At last Mary agreed to sell the farm and move to Chicago.

It takes more than distance to escape a nagging conscience. For more than six years he never laughed, almost never smiled. He relied more and more on liquor to blur his memory of the dying man's accusing eyes. There is an ounce of remorse at the bottom of every bottle, and Dick's mornings were times of horror. The only escape he knew was in more whiskey.

He concealed the story of the deathbed, but Mary knew some secret torture was destroying their lives. Each day was just a little worse than the one before.

Undernourished and living in foul surroundings, Mary developed tuberculosis. This added weight to Dick's burden of guilt. The accusing visions stayed with him even when he was drunk. He sat for hours at a time, muttering and crying to himself.

There was still another blow. Mary saved her discovery until Dick was sober, but he was on the shaking edge of delirium tremens when she broke the news.

"Dick, a terrible thing's goin' to happen."

"What are you gettin' at?" He glared at her from the fear-ridden depths of his hangover.

"We're—goin' to have a baby!"

This was disaster heaped on ruin. During the months that followed, Mary was too weak to leave her bed. Dick had been drinking to escape the memory of one sickbed. Now he was trapped in a room with another one. The association of ideas was so vivid he could barely force himself to walk near the bed.

As he sat in the room night after night, stupefied by liquor, the voice of a memory whispered endlessly in his brain.

"God forgive you, son. God forgive you."

Dick began talking back to the voice, denying his guilt. Mary heard that one-sided, disjointed argument and learned what haunted her husband.

When he was able to listen, she tried to reason with him.

"Dick—you didn't kill your father, did you?"

"No!"

"Well, then . . .?"

The thing at last was in the open and Ramey could talk about it. He thought it over, and then asked, "Mary, what does the Bible say about—killing?"

She got out the worn old Book and found the twentieth chapter of the Book of Exodus. Dick took it and read, *"Thou shalt not kill."*

So far so good. Then Mary was struck with a sudden thought.

"Dick, did you *want* to kill him?"

Guiltily, he muttered, "What difference does that make?"

She turned to the Gospel according to Saint Matthew and pointed to the twenty-first verse of the fifth chapter.

"Ye have heard that it was said by them of old time, Thou shalt not kill; and whosoever shall kill shall be in danger of the judgment: But I say unto you, That whosoever is angry with his brother without a cause shall be in danger of the judgment. . . ."

Dick flung the Bible to the floor and stormed out of the house.

After that, he was never completely sober. Time after time he resolved to save money for the baby's birth, but what little there was always went for liquor.

When Mary's time came, Dick faced the ordeal of attending her himself. He went out and fortified himself with whiskey, and when he staggered home the baby had already arrived. It was still alive, but Mary was dead. In Dick Ramey's brain, the whisper of his father's voice went on and on, mingled with the infant's crying.

"God forgive you, son. God forgive you."

Next day, the neighbors did what little they could to help. When the child died, soon after, it was buried beside Mary in Potter's Field.

Broken by guilt, loathing himself, Dick Ramey shuffled the streets for weeks in a nightmare of self-accusation. When the alcoholic fog lifted a little, only one thing made sense. He might better be dead. By the same reasoning he had once applied to his stricken father, he was already dead but merely breathing. Why prolong the matter further?

He stumbled back toward his room, planning to make death official with a piece of jagged bottle glass. As he went, he was aware of a vague and distant sound of chanting. The words were unintelligible to him, but it seemed to be a number of voices speaking together in chorus. He turned to see where it came from.

Down the street was coming the gospel wagon of the Pacific Garden Mission. As it rattled over the rough paving bricks, he saw it was filled with people. They were saying together the promise of Jesus, and as the wagon rolled nearer he could distinguish the words.

"For God so loved the world, that he gave his only begotten Son, that whosoever believeth in him should not perish, but have everlasting life."

Everlasting life—for a man who counted himself already dead.

There was no belief in Dick Ramey, but a fear of the finality of the grave made him pause and listen. When the wagon had passed him, he followed it slowly down the sidewalk.

At the door of the Mission he hesitated. There was a little printed sticker pasted on the glass. It read, "God Loves You."

Dick figured that wasn't true, but he went on inside. On the Mission wall he read the same words he'd heard on the street.

"For God so loved the world. . . ."

Back of the rostrum big block letters stated, "God Is Love."

Dick wanted to laugh at that, but he felt too much like crying. A little sweet-faced woman came up to him and said, "God loves you, my friend."

He looked up at a picture of Christ, then raised his fist and shook it wildly. There in the Mission chapel he began to shout.

"All right—if you love me, *prove* it! If you're so all-powerful and full of love, see what you can do about saving *me!* If you're so full of forgiveness, forgive me! I've got a load of sin that would bust your back! Go on—do it!"

He was sobbing when they led him into the old prayer room.

* * * * *

The transformation of Dick Ramey was sound, lasting and unmistakable. With his life surrendered to the Living Person of the risen Saviour, Dick knew in the very center of his being that he really was forgiven. He knew the load of sin that had broken him would not break his new Lord, because it had been carried to Calvary nineteen centuries earlier.

They found Dick a job as one of the guards in Chicago's famous Art Institute. He stayed there for many years, and much of his free time was spent working with troubled men at Pacific Garden Mission.

One famous preacher, visiting the Mission, was told about the old riverman and insisted on meeting him at once. He called on Dick at the Art Institute. While they strolled through the galleries together, Dick quietly told his story.

Speaking of that meeting later, the preacher said, "There we were, surrounded by the world's great masterpieces. But the most wonderful of all was that plain, quiet man in the dark blue uniform—because a masterpiece is simply, the work of the Master."

Jane

"... despised and rejected ..."

When Jesus said, "O ye of little faith," he spoke straight to the society in which we live. Faced with rising alcoholism, insanity and crime we look for human answers. The ones we find are always inadequate, simply because they are human. The churches may fail us too, not because we ask too much of Christianity, but because they expect too little of Christ. Perhaps the story of Jane will make it clear. It uses only her first name. You'll see why as you read.

JANE IS A SANE WOMAN, ACTUALLY AND LEGALLY. AS THE OLD joke goes, she has papers to prove it. She didn't set out to be a delinquent or a psychopath, but that's what she found herself. She knows what Paul meant when he wrote, *"but what I hate, that do I."*

There was one clear mark of trouble when she was twelve. Jane stole a quarter from her father, and her mother went into a rage over it. Many children make some small attempt at petty theft, but to Jane's mother it was a major crime. The beating was one to be remembered always. Many years later a psychiatrist blamed Jane's convulsions on an injury received that day.

Jane didn't want to be a thief or a delinquent. In fact, of all things, she wanted to take up the life of a religious. Her mother reacted with open scorn. When Jane mentioned a calling, the mother squelched it in a hurry.

"Religious life? You're not good enough for that! Forget it!"

But the need to serve God stayed with her. When she was sixteen, Jane took her ambition to a clergyman.

He said, "I advise you to forget it, Jane. You're just not the type."

"But why?"

"Too independent. You'd never learn to obey God."

"Then," she asked, "you think I'm not good enough to serve God?"

"Well—if you want to put it that way, yes. You need God, Jane. But I doubt if God needs you!"

Psychiatrists have a lot to say about "rejection." So did Jesus. He said, *"And whoso shall receive one such little child in my name receiveth me. But whoso shall offend one of these little ones which believe in me, it were better for him that a millstone were hanged about his neck, and that he were drowned in the depth of the sea."*

The clergyman had evidently read neither psychiatry nor the words of Jesus. The results were tragic.

Rejected by those who presumed to speak for God, Jane set out to live up to their estimate.

She headed out into a round of parties and drinking and boy friends, the more the merrier. When still very young, and purely for spite, she married a much older man. The results were all that could be expected. Any moment of any day of the eight years they were married could have been described as hell on earth. Jane's temper flared high. His temper flared even higher. He was a heavy drinker and a bitter man. Jane's nerves cried for whiskey, but there wasn't enough to deaden her misery. She went without sleep night after night, hating and fearing her husband. And still she longed for God. Sometimes she lay awake for hours, crying and then trying to pray. This enraged her husband most of all.

"You're a blasted female hypocrite! If there was any God, the church would fall down when you went in the door!"

"But I mean it, John. I *want* to go to church! Our son *needs* to go to church!"

"No wife of mine goes to church! And no son of mine will go to church except over my dead body!"

"Why, John? Why?"

"Because churches are a lousy racket. They talk about God when there isn't any God! They're out to get rich on suckers like you!"

"That isn't so! If there weren't any God, why would I want to go to church?"

"Because you're nuts! You've got a screw loose somewhere!"

"But I *want* to go back to church!"

"You're too big a sinner to go to church. You're nothing but a rotten hypocrite!"

Scenes like that were hard for Jane, but they were completely brutal for her five-year-old son. When the shouting began, he pressed himself against the wall and watched with eyes like those of a trapped animal. By the time he was six, the boy had lost his sunny disposition. He lived more and more within himself, somber and unresponsive.

It was for the boy's sake that Jane left her husband and took the boy to live with her mother. She found a job and a tiny room for herself.

Free to attend church, she did. But there was no comfort in the service. If anything, she felt closer to God alone in her room than she did in the big, arched sanctuary.

Her unhappiness and nervousness grew steadily more acute. When she visited the little boy, his troubled face haunted her for days afterward. She remembers one week when she was able to sleep only six scattered hours altogether. Still she tried to keep up with her job. This was impossible in her exhausted condition, and she was fired. Three times in one year she made sincere attempts at suicide. Twice she was saved by emergency treatment. The third time she failed to take a large enough dose of poison.

Guilt settled over her. She despaired of ever finding God. Her mother and a clergyman had told her she wasn't good enough for God. Now she told herself the same thing. And with this conviction established, she tried again to live up to the damning estimate. Jane began running around, trying to find forgetfulness in pleasure. But there was no relief; only new guilt.

Once, one night, unable to sleep, she beat on a·clergyman's door. When he sleepily opened it, she burst out crying.

"Help me! Please help me!"

He tried to collect his wits.

"What is it you want at this hour?"

"Peace with God."

"What? At this time of night!"

Jane begged, "Tell me how I can find peace with God. I feel so—so guilty all the time!"

The man thought of an answer.

"Do you go to church?"

"I did go. But I can't find any peace. Isn't there any way I can find God and peace?"

By now the man had gathered his thoughts.

"God has forgiven worse sinners than you—when they're

ready to stop sinning; when they're ready to make satisfaction for their sins. I think you have a guilt complex, but
you're not broken enough yet. Come back to church when
you're ready. Till then there's really nothing I can do.
Now, it's late and this is most irregular. Good night."

The door closed. Jane wandered away with her burden.

She was alone and helpless; unable to sleep, unable to
work. Within days she was committed to a state mental
institution.

There she vegetated. Her family had rejected her, and
there was no one to sign an authorization for shock treatment. Jane refused to sign for it herself, so she just remained locked up. She wasn't violent, merely disturbed
and helpless. Lying on her cot in a ward with other mental
patients, she prayed for hours at a time.

One friend came to call on her, and during those visits
they worked out a plan. The friend's husband posed as
Jane's uncle and arranged for her release. The scheme
was dishonest, but God was able to use even that for His
long-range purpose.

The hours spent in rest and prayer had calmed Jane a
little and she found work. Her son came back to live with
her. Then she lost him again, and for three years he was
kept in a juvenile home. During all that time, she paid for
regular psychiatric treatment out of her small salary. She
tried going back to church, but still there was no real
peace. Once more she tried suicide and once more was
rescued. After that attempt, she found another job and
again arranged for her son to live with her. Anxious to
make him feel at home and secure, she turned more and
more to God in prayer.

When Jane had trouble getting a decent apartment in a
new housing project, she couldn't possibly see the inter-
vening hand of God. But the apartment she finally *did*

get was so located that He could reach her through other people.

It was early in February of 1952 that her new next door neighbor knocked on Jane's door.

"I'm Mrs. Balker. I heard your son say your radio's burned out."

"That's right, and we miss it, too. My boy gets restless when we. . . ."

"Well, now wait." Mrs. Balker was full of old-fashioned neighborliness. "We always listen on Saturdays to a wonderful program called 'Unshackled.' Why don't you and the boy come over tonight and listen with us?"

Right then the program picked up two new listeners. Week after week, Jane and her son heard true stories of people whose lives had been surrendered to Christ and who had been transformed by His power. When she lay awake nights, Jane seemed to hear those voices with their quiet, convincing testimony.

"I'm a new man—inside and out."

"I don't need to drink anymore."

"I'm free."

"I'm forgiven."

"*Come unto me, all ye that labor and are heavy laden, and I will give you—rest.*"

Jane wondered more and more. Were these people *really* forgiven? They all talked as though it were so easy—just as though forgiveness was something *free*! She had been praying all her life—going to church, and she didn't feel forgiven at all. Each week there was a new story of someone "Unshackled," and each one said the same basic thing.

"I'm at peace!"

Jane had to know more about this. There was a little church across the street, and the pastor lived right next door. Jane took her problem to him.

When she had told her story, she said, "I don't feel forgiven at *all,* Pastor Tyler."

"But God is showing you the way He *can* forgive you, Jane. He's moving toward you through 'Unshackled' and Mrs. Balker."

"But I've gone to church hundreds of times and prayed my heart out. . . ."

"And God heard your prayers, Jane. Every one of them."

"Then why doesn't He forgive me?"

"Jane—do you know the Lord?"

"Certainly," she said. "I just told you. I've been to church and. . . ."

"But do you know Jesus Christ as your *personal Saviour* the way those people on 'Unshackled' know Him? Jane, God can't forgive you except through Christ personally."

Jane was getting impatient.

"Look," she said. "I want peace with God. I don't want to be converted to another religion. Religion and dogma and creeds and all those things are man-made. I want to know God!"

The pastor burst out laughing. Then he said, "Well, praise the Lord. You've finally seen the truth of it!"

"What do you mean by that?"

"Do you know Jesus Christ died for *your* sins, Jane?"

"Yes—I've always believed that."

"Then do you really want forgiveness? If you do, you can have it right now."

"Is it *that* easy?" she asked.

"Just that easy! Receive Jesus Christ as your personal Saviour and let Him forgive you. Let Him give you calm and quiet."

"You mean—right now?"

"Right now."

The calm and the quiet were real. For a week after she

received Christ as her own personal Saviour, Jane walked on air. She slept peacefully and deeply every night for seven nights, the first really refreshing sleep she had known in more than fifteen years.

Then her old fears began to come back. She wondered if she really *was* forgiven. Maybe she was just kidding herself. She listened again to "Unshackled" and wondered why she didn't feel as radiant as the people on the program sounded. Uncertain and frightened, she had to know more about this forgiveness. Next day, she wandered into the Pacific Garden Mission.

In the lobby a young nurse from the Mission Clinic spoke to her.

"Hello. Could I help you?"

"I don't know. I don't even know for sure why I came here. Except I listen to 'Unshackled' every Saturday, and last week I became a Christian."

The nurse, Lorraine Riley, was delighted.

"Why, that's wonderful," she said.

"That's what I thought too, at first. But now all the joy's gone, and I feel like nobody cares about me, and. . . ."

Lorraine said, "Hey, now. Wait a minute. There's nothing to cry about. *We* all care about you, and so does God."

"But everything seems so gloomy now."

"It doesn't *have* to seem gloomy. But don't expect to live on a pink cloud all the time, either."

Jane sniffed, "But they all sound so happy on 'Unshackled'."

"You mean—just before Lucille Becker starts playing the 'Lord's Prayer' on the organ?"

"Yes—they're all so peaceful, and life sounds just like a bed of roses."

Lorraine said, "Life is never a bed of roses—for any of us. But it can be triumphant. You're just a baby starting

out with Christ in a new life. But you'll find that no matter
what happens, good days and bad, He always gives us the
strength and the grace we need to be peaceful in the midst
of all the un-peaceful things that go on around us."

"Is that true?"

"It's *gospel* true. And all of us here at the Mission want
you to know how glad we are to have you with us—any
time at all—while you're learning to walk with Jesus."

After that, Jane called often at Pacific Garden Mission.
There was always someone willing to talk over her troubles
and pray with her. Sometimes it was Lorraine Riley, sometimes Elaine Chabonoff of the Women's Division. They
always found time for Jane. And at last there came a day
of real crisis. Jane was crying when she came to Elaine.

"I'm scared, Elaine. The psychiatrist I've been going to
made me face something I just can't go through with."

"Then we'll just have to give it to the Lord. What is it
you can't face?"

"I've started—having convulsions! The doctor says it's
because of a blow I got when I was a child. My—mother
beat me for stealing a quarter."

"And what is it you can't face?"

"The doctor said I should—I should. . . ." She broke
off, crying too much to continue.

Elaine said, "Easy does it, Jane. Now tell me, what did
the doctor tell you to do?"

"He said I should—tell my mother off—write her a
letter and—lay her out good for what she did!"

"Does he think that might release you?"

"I guess so. But Elaine—I can't write to her. I'm scared!"

Elaine laughed. "I'm not surprised. I'd be scared to do
anything that un-Christian, too."

"Un-Christian?"

"That's right. You're a Christian now, Jane. That means
that God has forgiven you—of everything. If you have an

old grudge against your mother, you have to forgive *her*. All the way. No reservations. That's Christ's way. I think it will work much better than telling her off and hanging on to your resentment."

That wasn't so easy either. But they prayed together, and when they rose from their knees, Jane was ready to write her letter. She had forgiven her mother before God. Now she could reach out to her mother with that forgiveness.

The letter she wrote went a second mile. It didn't merely forgive. It *asked* forgiveness for all she had ever done to hurt her mother. Jane wrote and waited, but no answer came. So she went another mile—and still another. She sent three letters in all. And before writing each one, she went crying to Elaine. Each time Elaine pointed out that they had committed the matter into God's hands.

The third letter brought a reply. And Jane's seizures stopped!

When Jane's own story was dramatized on "Unshackled," she sat in the studio with her son; she a poised and cheerful woman and he a normal and friendly teen-ager. It was hard to imagine that they might have ended up a suicide and a juvenile delinquent.

Jane tells of her last friendly visit to her psychiatrist. She says he just shook his head in wonder. He couldn't really figure out what had happened to her. But he is a sincere man and didn't even question that something *had* happened.

Jane says, "Now I can understand the others on 'Unshackled.' Because I know God, through Christ, *'hath not given us the spirit of fear, but of power, and of love and of a sound mind'*."

And she says, "Christ is all sanctity—but He is all sanity, too."

Keith Engle

. . . no bottle . . . no battle

NOTHING IS MORE HEARTBREAKING THAN TO BE A heartbreaker. Does that seem like doubletalk? Ask Keith Engle. He made a career of being a Casanova. The everyday word is "wolf."

Like all hit-and-run lovers, Keith was trying to prove something to himself. He was trying to reassure himself that he was really quite a fellow, trying to find something special just over the next hill. But what he looked for, he never found. And what he found, he didn't even know he was looking for.

By the time he was nineteen, Keith was a fast worker. He had to be to steal Marge away from her escort. It all happened in a roadhouse. Marge and her date were standing beside the dance floor. She was pretty and brunette, and she glanced at Keith with just the faintest speculative look. That was all he needed. He eased closer and spoke to her escort.

"Give me an introduction to your lady friend, chum?"

"No."

"No? Then I'll have to do it myself. Hello, Miss."

She smiled very slightly.

"Well—hello."

66

Her escort snapped, "Beat it, Engle!"

"Later, Bub. That wasn't much of an introduction, but it'll do."

He turned again to the girl.

"Did you hear the man say my name? It's Engle. Keith Engle."

"Mine's Marge." The smile was warmer now. "Hello, Keith."

From that moment she was Keith Engle's date. That night and for months afterwards. And for a little while she made him feel secure.

Keith needed that secure feeling. It was something he had never known at home. His father was a miner, working in the coal fields close to the Missouri border of Iowa. There were five boys in addition to Keith, and a houseful of uncles as well. Whenever the whiskey left any money to spare, the uncles paid board.

Though his father drank, too, it never seemed as bad to Keith as it did with his uncles. He admired his father tremendously. But with his love went the shaky inner insecurity that comes to a boy whose father drinks.

At sixteen Keith had learned to drink too. Sometimes the whiskey helped hide his fears. Then he discovered that romantic conquest was another prop to his ego.

Hence, Marge.

And when Marge wasn't looking, there was Jean. Then Jean died. That shook Keith badly, but there were others to take her place.

Now Keith says, "The more girls I had crazy about me, the more I felt maybe I wasn't such a bad guy after all. It helped stabilize that shaky place down inside me. Made me feel strong—when I was really afraid."

But in those days Keith hadn't seen that, and the conquests went on and on.

There was still Marge, the possessive one. She was often jealous and angry and mortified, but she clung fiercely. The night they finally broke up was one to remember. Keith had kept her waiting more than two hours. Then he showed up half drunk. Marge was furious.

"Do you know how long I've been waiting for you, Keith Engle? No—don't try getting mushy. I could smell you the minute you came in the door!"

"What are you talkin' about?"

"Whiskey—that's what I'm talking about!"

"So what? I just had a couple of drinks on the way."

"Just a couple! Does it take liquor to give you nerve enough to walk in here?"

"Skip it, Marge. Skip it!"

"I'll bet you weren't drinking alone. Not you!"

"That's right. I had three other dates between seven and nine o'clock. They stand in line for me! Does that please you?"

"Would you do anything to please *me*? You don't love me one bit and I know it!"

Here was the possessiveness. It made Keith boil with resentment.

"Marge, don't you have any pride at all?"

"Not where you're concerned. I'll keep you, Keith Engle, if I have to kill you to do it!"

"Look, pest. Why don't you cool off? It's too hot to fight."

"I'd be hot too, in that fancy jacket!"

Keith laughed at her.

"Sore because it's new, aren't you?"

"No I'm not! I'm sore because you bought it with the fifty dollars I lent you! That's why I'm sore, you deadbeat!"

She grabbed the sleeve of his coat and began to pull.

"Take off that coat, do you hear me? Take it off!"

"Okay." He slipped out of the jacket. "There. Does that make you feel any better?"

"No, but *this* will!"

Dragging the new jacket by the sleeve, she ran outside to the gravel walk. Crying hysterically, she began stamping the coat into the rough stones and cinders.

"Marge! Stop that!"

Keith caught her arms and tried to quiet her. She broke loose, raked him with her fingernails, and kept on stamping the new jacket.

"This'll be *one* coat you won't wear to impress some other woman. I don't lend you money to make a fool of me! I'll make rags out of this thing first!"

She picked the ruined garment up and flung it at him. He caught it, then stood looking at her with pure hate. She knew what was coming before he spoke.

"All right, Marge. This does it. Now I'll give you something you can *really* yell about! And you can yell by yourself. I'm leaving—for good!"

There were plenty of other girls, and Keith found them. First he thought he was in love with Nancy. That ended just as with Marge. The only difference was that Nancy was blonde.

Also, as it turned out, Nancy was easier to get away from. Just when Keith was growing sick of her clinging, the draft board called him.

In the Army Keith shifted his drinking habits from whiskey to beer. His other traits were unchanged, and he soon found a WAC named Julie. Julie was smarter than the others. When she learned that Keith was spreading his affections around, she told him not to come back. For a very few days Keith found himself actually wishing Julie was a little more possessive. It took a lot of drinking and another girl to get her out of his mind.

After the war he found Marie, but by this time his drinking was becoming a serious problem. Marie had a little son, and because Keith was drunk so much of the time she decided to send her boy to live with a grandmother. This looked too permanent, so Keith broke up with her too.

The liquor began to crowd out his romantic life. It appeared he might become free of girls by concentrating on the bottle.

About that time he was called home where his father was dying of tuberculosis. Keith's father had found time to think things out while lying in bed, and he had some advice to offer. They talked a good deal together about this business of being free.

"You're not free, son," his father said. "You just think you are."

Keith was a little drunk, but willing to listen.

"What do you mean?"

"You won't be really free until you get free of the thing that makes you chase around and drink—and look for freedom."

"But what am I looking for? What is it I want? I've tried everything?"

"Everything except God, son."

This from his father? Keith tried to protest, but his Dad continued.

"Yep, Keith. Your old Pop has turned back to God. I've done a lot of thinkin' since I've been sick, and I've got my life straight with Jesus Christ again."

"Well that's okay as far as it goes, Dad. But it seems like I've always got to have somebody to love me—somebody on my side. And I mean a *real person*."

"Keith—Jesus Christ *is* a real person. That's what I've been finding out. You think it over, son."

They had a good many talks like that, and Keith's father's last request was that he would stop drinking.

The night his father died, Keith was drunk. At the funeral he was even drunker, and he danced all that night at a roadhouse. The girl was named Phyllis.

She never became possessive. She had no time, because two weeks after the funeral Keith landed in the veterans' hospital at Waukesha, Wisconsin, with tuberculosis.

Here there was nothing to drink, no way of hiding from himself. There was only the bed, and pain, and loneliness.

Complete rest was essential. For recreation there was only a set of headphones connected to a radio receiver. The circuit offered a choice of three stations. One night, terribly bored, Keith dialed a dramatic program that caught his attention. It was about a man who loved the bottle as much as Keith did. Keith listened with thirsty sympathy, but the story ended in a surprising way. It made Keith think of his father. The man escaped from alcoholism through turning to Jesus Christ. The announcer said it was a true story.

Keith was scornful of the ending, but somehow it stuck in his mind. The next week he listened from the very beginning to this program called "Unshackled." The story was about a man with wanderlust. He got so mean and shifty that his wife almost left him. Then, sure enough, he got "Unshackled" too. And he gave the credit to Christ.

Keith figured that was just a little too easy, but again the announcer said it was true. Keith muttered, "Phooey," and switched off the headphones.

Next week he started watching the clock four hours before the program was due. That was May 12, 1951. The true story on "Unshackled" was about Jimmy the Rat, a seventeen-year-old kid who broke loose from dope. At the end of the program, the announcer gave the reason. He said it was, "through a personal encounter with Jesus Christ, the Son of God."

Keith hung on every word as the announcer went on.

"We do not offer a religion or a philosophy—we offer the Person of Jesus Christ. When a man's life is torn apart, he does not want the God-principle. He wants a personal Saviour. Someone who is personally interested in him. Turn right now in repentance to the Person of Jesus Christ, Who waits to receive you as His own. Repentance means turning your back on your old life and receiving by faith the new life He has for you. Turn now—right where you are—to Christ."

The program ended, but the words kept repeating themselves in Keith Engle's brain. Hours went by and sleep refused to come, but the words were as clear as though the radio was still turned on.

He remembered his father saying, "You've tried everything except God, son."

The words of the announcer kept coming back. "Turn now—right where you are—to Christ. Right where you are!"

It was very late when Keith, staring up at the dark ceiling, began to pray in a hoarse whisper. He was making his Eternal agreement with Christ as his *personal* Saviour.

"Jesus, You wouldn't create me and not help me out of this mess would you? I'm turning my back on everything but You, God—from now on! And I'm not kiddin'. I'm awful sick—and I want a drink, You know that—but here I am. Come and help me. Save me, for Jesus' sake."

Keith thought a minute and then added, "Amen."

Then he fell into a deep sleep.

In the morning he felt so good about it he just had to tell someone. The man in the next bed was openly scornful.

"What? You did *what*, Engle?"

"Like I told you. About two-thirty this morning I started praying. I told Christ I was on His side from now on."

"Well, that's fine. Did He say, 'thank you,' Engle?"

"I mean it! I'm a Christian now!"

"Do tell? When do you start preachin'?"

Keith began getting red. "No, it's true. I don't exactly understand it; but honest, I feel *different*."

"Well, don't pick up your bed and walk out with it." The man laughed at his own joke. "That bed still belongs to the V.A."

There was an interruption, but it only added to Keith's embarrassment. An ambulatory patient came over with a fistful of tickets on a baseball pool. Keith and his neighbor had been gambling on the pool daily.

"Okay, men. I'm sellin' nothin' but lucky tickets today. Who's gonna get rich on the ball game?"

Keith's neighbor sat up in bed and folded his hands in the best clerical manner.

"Please go away, sir, with those *nasty* gambling tickets. Parson Engle here wouldn't approve. Besides, we're about to have our prayer meeting."

The pool promoter was confused.

"Hey—what's eatin' you guys? What gives with the prayer meetin'?"

Keith knew he'd better explain.

"Knucklehead's giving me a hard time because—well, because I—I became a Christian last night."

"A Christian? What were you before—a Hindu?"

"No—now, look. You know that radio program from Chicago? The one they call 'Unshackled'? You listened to it. You know what I'm tryin' to say!"

He waited for a reaction. The two men looked at each other and then back at Keith. He wasn't violent, so they decided it wasn't worth bothering about. The promoter resumed his sales talk.

"Okay, that's fine! Now then, how many tickets you want to take?"

Keith hesitated and his neighbor spoke up.

"Look, Keith. I'll buy one and you buy one, huh?"

"Yeah, Engle," said the promoter. "God is love. Are we your pals or ain't we?"

"Okay," Keith said. "I'll take it."

He lay back, exhausted by the conversation. A few moments later a stabbing pain made him cry out, and he collapsed completely. After a quick examination, the doctors decided on immediate surgery to check the relapse. Ribs would have to be cut away. In Keith's condition only a local anaesthetic was possible.

Waiting to be taken to surgery, Keith prayed aloud.

"Lord, stay with me! I'm Your's now, and there won't be any more half-way stuff or fence straddling. Forgive me for all the things I've done. . . ."

He thought of something, paused, and put that in his prayer, too.

". . . even the baseball pool, Lord. Because I know even that's gambling . . . and I want to be changed *all* the way."

A moment later they wheeled him to surgery for a tough, exhausting operation. He was conscious throughout.

Keith says, "I'd only known Jesus Christ a matter of hours, but I went *through* that pain *with* Him. The doctors and nurses did a lot of buzzin' about it. They knew I was hurtin'—and so did I. But I was *held* in a kind of peace I didn't know was possible. The pain was there, but so was Christ—and I was peaceful. They didn't expect me to pull through—especially afterward, when I developed yellow jaundice. And when I lay there day after day, with the needles in my arms, the doctors and nurses were puzzled. It seemed to them I wasn't fighting at all. They wanted me to fight, and I knew what they meant, all right. But they didn't seem to catch what *I* meant."

One of the nurses tried to encourage him.

"Engle, you can't give in to this thing. You've got to fight. Don't give up!"

"You—just don't—get it, honey. I'm just—restin' in the Lord's arms. He's—got everything—under control."

That evening at supper the nurse told another nurse named Lois about Keith.

"I'm worried, Lois. This patient's gone nuts on religion or something."

"Religion—what kind?"

"I don't know. Something about a radio program called 'Unshackled.' Lois, he's going through pain that would make anyone else wild. And he just lies there and smiles."

"I think I'd like to see him," Lois said. "Do you mind?"

"No, of course not. It's Keith Engle. Ward B, bed 6."

When Lois approached his bed, she was careful to be very quiet, but Keith was wide awake.

"Hello, there—Keith?"

"Hi."

"Keith—I hear you love the same Lord I do."

"Jesus—Christ?"

"Yes. Are you a—new Christian, Keith?"

"Yeah. You too?"

"Not so new, but I'm a Christian. My name's Lois."

"Hi, Lois."

"Keith—don't worry about fighting. Just rest in the Lord. I'll pray for you."

"Honest?"

"Honest. I think it'll do *me* a lot of good."

Keith smiled. "Go on!"

"I mean it," she said. "You're taking Jesus Christ at His word—and it *shows*. That gives *me* courage."

"You're not kidding me?"

"No, of course not. I'm on duty tonight, Keith. I can pray all night long."

And she did—all night long.

Lois kept right on praying through the months of Keith's recovery. They studied the Bible together, and while his body grew stronger Keith grew spiritually, too.

They're still praying together, and their children are learning to pray with them. Lois, the nurse, is now Mrs. Keith Engle.

Keith has found what he didn't even know he was looking for. And he says, "This is living! No bottle—no battle. The minute you get over on the side of Christ, you'll find out the Son of God has actually been on your side all the time."

Alice Parsons

. . . who smiled only once

LOUISE HALL'S STORY WAS DRAMATIZED ON "UNSHACKLED," and that broadcast brought her a blind date. Nothing romantic, but a frightening appointment with a correspondent who described herself as, "a rude, unhappy, sinful old woman."

The people whose stories are broadcast often get letters from listeners. Some are merely expressions of good will. Others ask for advice or prayer. This letter was in a class by itself. Something in the story of Louise's transformation from a bitter, aggressive, hard-talking fighter-against-the-world to a calm and dedicated servant of Christ had reached out with a strange appeal to the crabbed old woman, Alice Parsons. But it took Louise many uncomfortable months to discover what that "something" was.

Waiting now on the Harrison Street platform of the Chicago subway, Louise re-read the old woman's letter.

. . . I did not even want to listen to your story on the radio. But since I did listen, I find myself hoping that you will write . . . and I might . . . talk with you face to face.

Louise knew it wasn't for her to choose how the Lord might use her and the broadcast. She had answered the

77

letter, and by mail they had agreed to attend the service
at Pacific Garden Mission. The meeting place was to be the
subway station.

Waiting in the dank, echoing tunnel, Louise knew she
was actually afraid; afraid to meet this self-described,
"rude, sinful old woman." While she prayed for poise, a
train thundered in and squealed to a stop. Louise tried to
get out of the way of the crowd pouring past her. Moving
aside, she bumped into a tall, grim-looking woman with a
set, motionless face. They stared at each other for a moment. Every hard line in the gaunt, bony face said
something repellent—something Louise wanted to run
from! She turned and took three quick steps away, stopped,
tried to collect herself—and then turned back.

She tried to smile as she said, "I hope you don't think
I'm rude, but I'm supposed to meet someone on the station
platform and. . . ."

The woman answered coldly.

"I'm Alice Parsons."

They stood for a moment; two tall women. Then Louise
took Alice Parsons' arm and they climbed the long stairs
to the street above. The subway exit is less than a block
from the Pacific Garden Mission. When they reached the
surface, Alice Parsons spoke in a level, grating voice.

"I wish you'd let go of my arm, Mrs. Hall."

"Oh, I'm sorry." Louise was embarrassed. "I didn't. . . ."

"It's all right," the old woman snapped. "I just don't
like people to touch me."

"I understand."

"I doubt if you do. But that's the way I am."

During the Mission service, it was hard to know what
Alice Parsons was thinking. For Louise it was pure agony.
When she held a songbook for them to share, the old
woman looked away. When she held it for herself alone,

she caught Mrs. Parsons watching to see if she meant to share it.

During the invitation, Louise asked if she wanted to accept Christ. The lined face hardened.

"I've had enough of this, Mrs. Hall. Let's go."

That was their meeting. At home, Louise asked the Lord what it was all about. She prayed, "Lord, I'm willing to have You use me in any way You want."

Willing to go ahead until every door was shut, she wrote a note to her strange acquaintance. An answer came at once. That called for a reply and thus started a clumsy, limping correspondence that went on for months. Alice Parsons always wrote coldly, and Louise wished more than once the whole business might end. But Muriel, Louise's teen-age daughter, was deeply interested.

Louise had asked for the old woman's telephone number. The reply was a flat refusal, and this puzzled Muriel even more than it did her mother.

"Why, mother? Why do you suppose she won't give her number?"

"I don't know, Muriel. I don't understand her at all!"

"But why did God trust her to you in the first place?"

Louise shook her head. "I've wondered the same thing. I wish I could turn her over to someone who could really help. But she won't talk to anyone else."

Time passed and they grew no closer. There was not a hint of why Mrs. Parsons had made that first overture, yet she still wouldn't drop Louise. Once or twice they met for dinner in a restaurant. One night, as they parted, the old woman seemed to thaw a little.

She said, "I've had a nice evening, Mrs. Hall."

"I'm glad," answered Louise. "So have I."

"You don't need to say that." Alice Parsons at least wasn't devious. "Christians like you shouldn't lie."

"I know I'm not helping you any, but I can at least be your friend. And I want to be."

"You're good to come such a long distance."

"I don't mind," replied Louise. "I ride the train to the Loop every day. I'm used to it."

"Will you come back next week?"

"Why—yes, if you want me to."

"We'll have a bite to eat at my place then. I'll show you some quilts I've made."

This seemed like progress. Louise prayed and wondered what her next move should be. Perhaps the Lord was saying, "You just stay in position, Louise. In time I'll reach her heart." If that was it, Louise was willing to stay in position.

On the way to Alice Parsons' flat the following week she bought a bunch of spring flowers. The old woman opened the door, looked at the green-wrapped package, and almost grabbed it.

"Flowers!"

"Yes," Louise explained. "They looked so pretty, and I. . . ."

"Flowers for me!" Her laugh was hard and short.

"With my love," said Louise.

"Come inside. You're a funny one, Mrs. Hall."

"Thank you," Louise laughed. "Am I?"

"You and your daughter must laugh together a lot, don't you?"

"Well, yes. But I think she's a lot more sensible than her mother?"

The woman was puzzled. "What do you mean by that?"

"Well, you see—Muriel's been a Christian since she was a child. She's grown up with Jesus Christ in her consciousness. I didn't. I grew up all pinched and bitter at life. I hated even the mention of God."

Alice Parsons' face hardened.

"So do I!"

There was a silence. Louise broke it.

"Don't you want to open the flowers?"

"Oh! Why—yes, I do."

She unwrapped the package and began arranging the blossoms in a pitcher. There was skill and taste in the way she worked with them.

"Hm—they're nice. Much obliged to you."

"You're a wonderful housekeeper, Mrs. Parsons," Louise said.

"Why don't you call me Alice? Am I too old?"

"No—and anyway, I don't know how old you are."

"That's true, and it's none of your business, but I'm sixty-seven. I know I look older. You don't have to tell me."

"Actually, your age would be hard to guess."

"I'm a hard woman, Mrs. Hall."

"Call me Louise. I want us to be friends."

"Why?"

"Because I want you to trust me. You're unhappy, and I'd like to help you turn over your entire life to Jesus Christ as I did."

"Oh! These flowers'll need water. Excuse me."

Alice's defenses were up again, but Louise was getting used to sudden changes of mood. When they sat down to dinner, the best napkins and china and carefully trimmed party radishes all showed how much of an occasion it really was. Louise tried another opening.

"Are there any members of your family still living?"

"I don't think I need to answer that."

"No," said Louise. "Of course you don't. Have you heard from your husband lately?"

"I must have been awfully talkative last time we were together. I didn't aim to talk about him."

"Aren't we friends, Alice? Why slam doors in my face?"

"Just don't like to have people nosin' into my life. I warned you I'm a rude old woman. Told you that in my first letter. I oughtn't to have written it at all!"

Louise said, "I'm not nosing, Alice. I'm just concerned about you."

"Care for some more salad?"

"Yes. I hope you'll make it again for me sometime."

Alice Parsons served it carefully before she spoke.

"With me so snippy, I don't expect you'll be back again."

"I will be if you'll invite me."

Mrs. Parsons hesitated. Then, "I'm sorry I cut you off. There's nothing to hide about my husband. He's a hopeless case, they say—at the veterans' hospital."

"I'm sorry."

"I—believe you are. And I've no call to be snippy. Seems like I get worse every year. It just looks like I'm so— *touchy!*"

She thought at length, trying to reach some sort of decision.

"Louise?"

"Yes, Alice?"

Another long pause. Then she spoke with a rush.

"Do you think a person could damn another person's soul to Hell?"

This was the last question Louise had expected.

"In your story—on the radio. You lost your temper at your boss, remember? And you told him—where to go! They didn't say it in so many words on the radio, but that's what really happened, isn't it? You *did* condemn his soul to eternal damnation, didn't you? Isn't that just what happened?"

Louise was amazed. She said slowly, "Yes, it is. The words I really used were too bad to use on the radio. But why is that so important to you?"

It's not easy to watch the floodgates open up on years of pent-up guilt. The next half hour was a difficult one for Louise, but she was learning why she'd been remaining in position all these months. Alice told what it was that had made her a hard appearing, inwardly frightened woman. It was the thing that had made her respond to Louise's story.

Sometimes very simple guilts cause tremendous grief. Alice Parsons had been orphaned as a young girl. An uncle took her in to work as his housemaid. He was a brutal man and treated her miserably. On the day she finally left his house, raging with anger, she had clearly and profanely comdemned his soul to Hell!

When Alice finished telling the story, she was weeping. "That was forty-five years ago. He's been dead for twenty years now. And every single day of all those years I've been—afraid! I'm afraid to die! I'm afraid I'll find him—there in Hell!"

Louise said softly, "I'm glad you've finally told me."

"You know what I'm talking about," the woman sobbed. "You did it, too!"

"Yes, Alice. But when we place our wicked lives in the hands of Jesus Christ—He forgives us and changes us. He *forgets* our sins, puts them behind Him. The Bible says so."

"Don't talk to me about God and the Bible!"

"Alice, listen. You couldn't send your uncle to—'Eternal damnation,' as you say. Each man is responsible for his own soul. And Jesus wants to forgive *you!*"

Alice Parsons was calmer when they parted that night, but apparently only because of human sympathy. She seemed to remain stubbornly separated from Christ.

A few weeks later Louise learned the woman was in a hospital, very ill with cancer. During the long hospitalization, Louise called on her again and again. Each time she found Alice bitter with fear and self-hatred, and always in pain. Louise was still willing to "remain in position" for the Lord to use her when He saw fit. She and her daughter prayed that He might show them how.

As so often happens, the call came when she was least ready to respond. She was in the midst of painting and decorating her new apartment. The night was hot. She was perched on a ladder and holding a dripping paint brush when the telephone rang. It was Muriel, her daughter.

"Mother—I'm calling from the old apartment. I guess you'd better draw on all the love you know, because the hospital just called. They want you to come right away."

"Oh—no!" Louise waved her arm emphatically. A shower of paint from the wet brush spattered the wall.

"It's Mrs. Parsons," Muriel said. "She's probably dying."

Two hours later, paint-free and neatly dressed, Louise Hall sat in the dimly lighted hospital room on the other side of town. Alice Parsons' eyes were closed. Her breathing was heavy and painful to hear. Louise felt more helpless than she ever had in her life. She prayed, "Lord, what do I do next?"

The nurse came in. Louise asked, "Is there any chance that she's conscious—that she can hear us talking?"

"Yes, there's just a chance. But she may never open her eyes again."

Louise dabbed cool water on the cracked, dry lips. There was no response. She dabbed, and prayed, and then cried softly. Suppose the old woman died that night? Would she go into the Presence of Christ, transformed at last by His Holy Spirit because she had made her peace with God? Or would she face her Creator, the just God, as she had described herself in that first letter, "a rude, unhappy, sinful old woman"?

Louise began to speak quietly but with deep conviction.

"Alice, do you know I'm here? Can you feel my hand on your head?"

The dying woman made no response.

"The Lord is my shepherd, I shall not want. Alice, the Lord is my shepherd because I follow Him by choice—my choice. But Alice, the same Lord is waiting right here— just one step away from Eternity—to be *your* Shepherd, too. Even though you walk through the valley of the shadow of death, He will be with you, Alice—if only you'll follow Him as your Saviour and your Shepherd. It isn't too late, Alice. You still can choose. It still isn't too late. . . ."

Forty-five long minutes Louise Hall stood by the bedside, talking about Jesus Christ. There was no response to encourage her. She kept on because it seemed she had to.

More minutes passed, and still her hand rested lightly on the old woman's forehead. Then the tired eyes opened and looked straight into her own.

"Alice—Alice Parsons! You know me, don't you?"

The labored breathing grew faster.

"You don't have to say anything, Alice. I can tell— because this is the first time I've ever seen you smile! It's all right with you and Jesus—isn't it?"

The smile was real. Tired, but triumphant in the face of death.

And so was the one faint, whispered word that Alice Parsons spoke. Louise had to bend close to hear, but it was unmistakable.

"Shep—shepherd!"

The eyes closed and the breathing slowed.

Alice Parsons was dead before morning. But Louise Hall remembers her going with real joy.

She says, "One thing I know. Alice Parsons was forgiven and walked right into the Presence of Jesus Christ that night—with her head up—smiling!"

E. E. Standish

... who found peace

"Calm Soul of all things! Make it mine
To feel, amid the city's jar,
That there abides a peace of thine,
Man did not make, and can not mar."
Matthew Arnold

STANDISH WAS A SUCCESS BY ANY POSSIBLE WORLDLY MEASURE. Not a sensation, but a solid, respectable, dependable man of business. Socially, he was more than acceptable. Suave and polished, he read enough to be a good conversationalist and was the sort of eligible bachelor people need to make their dinner parties successful. Business associates usually addressed him by his initials, "E. E." Friends called him "Stan."

Yet, when E. E. Standish, clean shaven, neatly dressed and prosperous, came picking his way among the derelicts on a Skid Row street he was neither sight-seeing nor slumming. He passed up the saloons, the peep-shows, the burlesque houses and the pawnshops. For him all these things offered neither an attraction nor a problem. He was looking for the Pacific Garden Mission. The need he took

86

with him was as great in its own way as the needs of any
of the shabby men on that miserable street.

Standish needed peace of mind. That's one way of
saying he was a typical product of our civilization. As his
need for peace became more apparent, he had tried most
of the world's ways for seeking it. One by one they had
failed him. Now quietly desperate, he was looking for
peace of mind in the last place you'd expect to find E. E.
Standish on any errand—in a Skid Row rescue mission.

The symptoms had been a long time showing up in
Stan. For a number of years, he was too busy winning
promotion even to think of peace of mind. He saw life
as a sort of scramble for prizes, with never enough of them
to go around. This forced him to hustle to get his. There
was the right fraternity in college, the right apartment at
the right address, the window seat on the suburban train,
the right promotion in the company, the right office with
the sunniest view, and the right secretary with the proper
regard for her employer's delicately balanced peace of
mind.

That secretary business may have been one of the first
warnings that Standish's peace of mind was a little *too*
delicately balanced. Lately, he'd been wondering. He
could remember the day he fired that girl who . . . what was
her name? That's right, it was Miss Meadows. He recalled
every detail of the way he'd handled the matter. She had
been closing her book when he spoke.

"Miss Meadows, harmony is of the utmost importance to
me."

"Yes, Mr. Standish."

She stood up and a faint wave of cologne drifted across
the desk. He didn't care for sweet cologne.

"I'm a little afraid you and I are—not going to make
it."

She was surprised and showed it. Standish wished people would learn to govern their reactions.

"Aren't you satisfied with my work, Mr. Standish?"

"Completely." He leaned back in the swivel chair and noted with satisfaction that there was no squeak from the well-oiled springs. "You're an excellent secretary, Miss Meadows."

"Well—then I don't know *why* you say we can't make it, Mr. Standish. I've never left the office while there was any work left to do, even when it meant staying overtime. Lots of days I've stayed overtime and haven't even told you about it!"

"I know, Miss Meadows. You're telling me things I already know, but. . . ."

She broke in. He always disliked being interrupted.

"I've even done some of your boss's work so you'd always have things ready for action the next day!"

"I'm perfectly aware of that, Miss Meadows. Self-defense is not at all necessary."

"But, why don't you. . . ."

He was quite willing to interrupt a painful scene.

"You must understand that harmony in my working conditions is of the utmost importance to me. Harmony, Miss Meadows—complete harmony! I happen to be a man who can't stand confusion. My work requires concentration, and I enjoy working hard. I'm sorry we haven't made the grade,. and I'll see that you get six weeks' severance pay and an excellent recommendation. But I'll have to ask you to resign as of today."

"How can you give me an excellent recommendation when you're firing me?"

"I'm not an unkind person, Miss Meadows. I want you to find another position—one where things will be harmonious. This isn't selfishness on my part at all. I'm simply concerned about the company's best interests. They'll best be served when I have peace of mind. And I know, Miss Meadows, what my environment must be."

The girl was about to cry. Standish noted the signs of tears with deep distaste.

She said, "But what do I do wrong? I think I have a right to know why I'm being fired! What have I done?"

He sighed at the need to perform an unpleasant duty.

"Just what you're doing at this moment, Miss Meadows."

"What?"

"Chewing your fingernails like a schoolgirl!"

He'd been right about the tears. Miss Meadows wailed and ran to the ladies' room. Later, when she had gotten hold of herself, he dictated the letter of recommendation. It was really rather glowing, he thought, though she sniffed a time or two. She asked no further questions and he was relieved. It saved him having to tell her about the cologne (much too sweet), and her annoying trick of clearing her throat gently each time she picked up the phone.

Miss Meadows asked to leave early. It was a relief to Standish to see her go. The day had been most unharmonious. When he cleared his desk that evening, he noticed more than the usual number of cigarette ends in the ashtray. There were several over his usual careful quota.

"Bad sign," he thought. "No harmony—no peace of mind."

He sat with an acquaintance on the suburban train. Still troubled, he told of the day's annoyances. The acquaintance was sympathetic.

"You're right, Stan. Those little things can jangle a guy's nerves."

"They certainly can. Play hob with a man's peace of mind."

Now, that's true, of course. If a man's peace can be wrecked, little things can surely do it. And once that man starts *fighting* to hold his peace of mind he's well on the way to *never* having any.

Later on there was another thing that might have been a symptom. Standish recalled that it stemmed from his annoyance over the tiresome train ride to and from the suburbs. He began looking for an apartment in town. One building seemed ideal. It was ten minutes from his office and the address had solid prestige. He studied it carefully from across the street, taking satisfied note of the neat little lawn (curb your dog), the glass-canopied entrance, and the quietly uniformed doorman.

Stan decided he might as well see the apartment and pay a deposit at once. He went briskly to the intersection and crossed over.

A newsboy stood on the corner near the building entrance.

"Getcher eevnin' papeyeeer! Read all abaat it! Getcher payper-eer!"

If lungpower sold papers, the boy was tomorrow's tycoon.

Standish had passed him and almost reached the entrance-canopy when a sudden thought struck him. He stopped, reflected, and went back to the paper boy.

"Paper, mister?"

"Why—yes." Standish fished for a coin and the boy slammed a folded paper securely under his arm. "Keep the change."

The newsie was impressed.

"T'anks, mister! You live in here?" He flipped a thumb over his shoulder at the apartment house.

"Well—not yet. But I'm thinking about it."

"Swell joint. Takes a lotta dough. I guess you ain't worried none about money, though."

Standish ignored that and got to the point.

"Tell me, son—do you sell papers here every evening?"

"Yep. Mornin's too, before school!"

"Hmm—well, good luck."

"Sure!" The boy turned away. "Paaayper! Getcher evenin' paper!!"

Stan went in and looked at the vacant apartment. As he'd feared, the windows were close to the newsboy's corner. The view was lovely, but the hawking was audible even eight stories up. Standish sighed. Money was no assurance of peace of mind. Harmony was hard to come by. He thanked the manager and left. The newsboy was still yelling when he reached the street.

In time, a satisfactory apartment turned up. There were no newsboys within two blocks.

Soon, however, Stan discovered that the location of his new quarters was entirely *too* convenient. Customers, out on the town for an evening of carousing, often thought of their old pal, "E. E."

The house phone frequently rang at odd hours of the night and well-brandied voices greeted him from the lobby. This always upset Standish, but customers must be catered to. He forced himself to say, "Why don't you come up for a drink?" The invitation was never refused.

"A drink" usually turned out to be half a dozen, and Stan was no drinker. To him, the noisy parties that stumbled into his apartment were most inharmonious. Still, business was business. He told himself this was the cross he had to bear.

But when one of his own nephews showed up after midnight and demanded not only a drink, but twenty dollars as well, Stan was furious. The intoxicated boy found this very amusing.

"Stan, old uncle—I can tell by the look in your left

eyebrow that you would like to murder me—in warm
blood! Very warm, my good kinsman, because it's fortif—
ah—forti-fried—fortifried with anti-freeze. Tha's very
funny, isn't it?"

"No," Standish said. "I don't find you amusing. In fact,
you're disgusting!"

"Tha's exshellent! Then perhaps you'll loan me twenty
dollars so I can be on my way?"

"No!"

"No? I'm dishappointed! In fact—I'm so dishappointed
I think I'll jus' lie down on your couch for a while—and
brood about it."

"No!"

The nephew ignored him grandly and stretched out
full length. Standish prodded him.

"Get up, you worthless drunken bum!" More prodding,
without result. "What do you want with the twenty?"

"If you musht know—I intend to purchase whishkey."

"That's the last thing you need in your condition . . .
Wait! Don't go to sleep! I'll never get you out of here if
you do!"

"Preshishely!"

Standish was desperate.

"All right, then. Take the twenty dollars and get out of
here. I'll pay blackmail before I put up with you!"

That happened five times. It was hard enough to have
peace of mind at the office. Now the apartment, his only
real refuge, was being invaded. He was losing precious
sleep. Standish lay awake all one night waiting for the
house phone to ring. It didn't, but by morning he was
exhausted. There was only one thing left to do. He packed
a few clothes and went to a hotel.

The first couple of nights he just slept. But once he'd
caught up on his rest the room seemed too small for his—

peace of mind. Standish worked hard all day, kept his new address a secret, and spent the evenings pacing up and down between the dresser and the bed. Before the end of the week, his restlessness drove him to the lobby to find companionship.

He struck up a conversation with a man named Simmons. Simmons was a good listener. Within ten minutes Stan was telling his troubles in a most uncharacteristic way.

Simmons said, "Too bad. It's a shame you had to leave your home and move into a hotel."

"A shame? It's terrible. I don't know what's happened to me lately. Sometimes, when I hit the bed at night, I wish I'd just sleep away."

"That bad, eh?"

"And the strange thing is that I've always lived a decent, law-abiding, respectable life. I've got all I need for security. I don't gamble. I don't drink. I watch my cigarettes—even coffee! But people won't let me have any peace!"

"That's the great problem of the age we live in."

Standish nodded. "You're right. There just doesn't seem to be peace anywhere. I've traveled to all the so-called peaceful places. I've read books. I've tried to hold right thoughts—but peace is always out of reach. No harmony!"

"Maybe we're all expecting a miracle of some kind."

Standish laughed. "Well, the age of miracles is past."

Simmons was silent. Then he said, "I wonder if it is?"

"What do you mean? Miracles?"

"A *kind* of miracle," Simmons said. "Some friends have been telling me about a place here in town where miracles —of a sort—happen every day."

"If you're talking about peace—it must be the morgue."

"No. I laughed when they told me. It's a Mission."

"A Mission?" Standish was confused. "You mean— converting the heathen savage?"

"Uh—not exactly. We seem to have heathens quite close to home. This place is on South State Street, down in Skid Row."

"Oh, one of those!" Stan was relieved. "You mean—soup and salvation. Bible-thumping and hymn-singing."

"Something like that. But these friends of mine claim they heard ex-drunkards and ex-gamblers—even a murderer—stand up and vow they'd found what *you're* looking for."

"Peace of mind?"

"That's right. Sounds fantastic, doesn't it?"

It certainly did. But it stuck in Standish's mind and he couldn't shake it loose. Later on, when he'd paced his room for a couple of hours and felt more un-harmonious than he ever had in his life, he decided to find out. Stan told himself it was just curiosity—and besides, he had time to kill. He had long ago marked religion off his list of ways to find peace.

That's how E. E. Standish came to Pacific Garden Mission.

During the service, he tried to hang on to his aloof, skeptical attitude. But this wasn't preaching. It was testimony, from men and women whose faces vouched for the truth of what they said.

Over and over again they spoke of having—joy! Almost every one mentioned having peace of mind. They usually described it as, "the peace that passeth all understanding." But in spite of the unfamiliar words, Standish could see they were talking about the thing he lacked. He began feeling uncomfortable and tried to resist the growing weight of testimony.

"This is ridiculous," he thought. "These people are boasting! This is rank, ignorant egotism dressed up to look like religious experience. It's utter pomposity!"

Still, he knew that if these people were crazy, it would

be a relief to have their kind of insanity. The peace they had was worth anything. But *he* couldn't stay in a place like *that*!

Standish hurried outside and hailed a cab. He had to be alone, to think and recover his conventional perspective.

The hotel room was just as he'd left it, but now he was uncomfortably conscious of the Gideon Bible on the dresser. He'd seen hundreds of them, of course, but this one refused to be ignored. He knew there was nothing in it for him. He was an upright, respectable man. He had no sins to confess!

When he picked up the Bible, it fell open to the Book of Romans. Standish began to read, and as he read he sank to his knees by the bed.

"There is none righteous, no, not one: there is none that understandeth, there is none that seeketh after God. . . . Their throat is an open sepulchre; with their tongues they have used deceit; the poison of asps is under their lips. . . . Destruction and misery are in their ways: and the way of peace have they not known."—The way of peace they have not known!

There on his knees, he began to pray.

"God! In the name of Jesus Christ, forgive me for my selfish life and give me peace. . . . give me *peace*!"

* * *

It was daybreak when Standish rose from his knees. During the long hours of prayer, he had seen himself for the first time, not through his own eyes, but through the eyes of Jesus Christ. He saw that E. E. Standish had been playing God. And he knew at last that without Christ the ingredients of peace simply weren't in him. He knew, too, that at last he had been *given* peace, because *in* him now lived the Person of God Himself.

That day showed him the reality of his transformation.

Though he'd had no sleep, his day's work was, of all things, harmonious. He didn't have to protect his precious self.

That night, still without sleep, he was back at Pacific Garden Mission. E. E. Standish, dignified business man, had his own story to tell there of, "the peace that passeth all understanding."

That was only a beginning. Night after night, for the remainder of his life on earth, Stan joined his ex-derelict friends with the scarred faces, telling the true story of how *he* found peace—when he permitted Jesus Christ, the Son of God, to find him. He always remained suave and respectable, socially acceptable. But more than that—he was *poised* and *peaceful*.

Art Petznick

"... and the tongue (shall) sing. ..." (Isaiah 35:6)

THEY TELL AN OLD STORY, AND NOT A VERY FUNNY ONE, OF a brain surgeon with palsy. Art Petznick's true story is fully as strange and completely true. It's the story of a stammerer who became a preacher. If that sounds like a joke or a miracle, be sure it's no joke. As for miracles, Art Petznick has lived by miracle for some time now.

He was born on a farm in the rich wheat lands of Canada, and until he was eight or nine years old Art's speech was as good as any other little boy's. Then he developed the impediment that was to mark his life.

We're told that stammering is usually caused by emotional problems. Art knows the answer in his own case. His father was an inconsistent and violent man. Art lived in the constant turmoil of a house dominated by his father's unpredictable temper.

The senior Petznick was a "Sunday Christian." He went to church and insisted that his children go with him, but left God in the pew and forgot all about Him until seven days later. Little Art heard things like, "be ye kind, one to another," and, "love one another," but they never carried over into life at home. There his father took over and pushed God aside. Church, it seemed, was one thing

97

and life another. Art couldn't see where they had much
connection.

He became a smart-alec, rebellious kid. The only proof
that he *really* cared was that clumsy, embarrassing, stammering speech. It was the mark of a boy with nothing
solid to rely on.

After high school he stayed on the farm for several years.
During that time his church-attending, Sabbath-observing
father taught him to drink. This was one lesson Art
learned readily. But when the boy played ball on Sundays
or went to community dances, he was in trouble. His
father, who had swallowed the camel of liquor, strained at
a gnat. Big as Art was, he was whipped for such scandalous
conduct.

Mrs. Petznick bore the load of trying to hold her family
together. In the face of her husband's contradictions and
violent temper, she acted as a buffer between the man and
his children. This divided Art's loyalties and magnified his
insecurity.

Things came to a head when Art went to a village dance,
got drunk, and wound up in a fight. His father heard of it
and was furious.

"What kind of a son do I have? This is a Christian home
—and I expect you to remember it!"

"B-bb-but—anyb-body m-might g-gg-get into a . . ."

"Not my son! And I'll see to it from now on!"

Art's mother tried to intervene.

"Let's try to be calm about this, shall we?"

"Calm! Calm, you say! When this young hoodlum goes
out and gets in drunken brawls—in public!"

"And who taught him to drink?"

"Don't try to change the subject! The boy's a disgrace
and you know it. He'll either change his ways, or he can
get out!"

"Please—try to be sensible about this and . . ."

"I'll thank you to leave this matter to me!"

He turned back to his son. "Now then, Arthur, what do you have to say for yourself?"

"P-pp-plenty!"

"What kind of talk is that? P-pp-plenty! For the love of Pete, talk like a man. What do you suppose people would think of me if I talked like a teakettle?"

This was one more cruelty than Art could take. He was almost in tears as he replied.

"I know w-what I th-th-think ab-bout y-you! You s-said t-tt-to ch-change m-my w-ways or g-get out. And I'm g-gettin' out! F-for g-gg-good!"

The words were halting, but the resolution was firm.

Art crossed the border into the States and headed for Florida. Jobs weren't plentiful for a man with a pitiful tongue. He looked for the little odd ones that didn't call for talking. They didn't pay much, and his progress was slow.

It was the early part of the great depression. As that winter set in, jobs became harder and harder to find. In those days we talked about "the great army of the unemployed," and Art Petznick was soon fighting the battle of the breadline. He thumbed his way to Chicago and began drifting on Skid Row. Odd jobs came and went. Sometimes Art had a little money. When that happened, he drank.

He was pouring them down in a speakeasy when a hard looking character struck up a conversation.

"You're too smart a kid to be drinkin' that cheap hootch. Lemme buy you a shot of good liquor."

Art was much too smart to talk when he didn't have to. He just grinned and nodded and grunted his acceptance. The man slammed his palm down on the bar.

"Hey—give my pal here a double shooter of real whiskey. Right off the boat!"

The new bottle actually had a label on it. Art was impressed.

"Just driftin', kid?"

"Yeah."

"Jobs are mighty scarce, ain't they?"

"Yeah."

"You broke?"

"Yeah."

"You don't talk much, do you?"

"Nope."

The barkeep had finished pouring the whiskey. Art's new acquaintance indicated the glass.

"There ya are. Put that down and things'll look better!"

"Th-thanks."

Art drank quickly.

"You sure don't talk much, do you?"

"Unh-unh."

"I can see that. Then you're probably the man I'm lookin' for. Here, lemme buy another one of those double shots. We got things to talk about."

The man was a gambler. He sold Art on the proposition that they could make good money gambling with suckers. But Art turned out to be the chump. As a gambler he was a failure.

By the time he was twenty-three, he was a member in good standing of the Grant Park hobo fraternity. In those days of mass unemployment, Chicago's park system included a good sized "bum jungle." It was home to Art. He learned to dig up his contribution to the community stew pot or do without. He also learned how to meet the increasing demands of alcoholism with canned heat or anything else that might yield a little jag.

Life in the jungle was too disappointing to face with a clear head. Drinking deadened the pain of owning nothing, belonging to no one, and going nowhere.

Things began moving in Art's life in October of 1931. One night, he was slumped in an old chair in the back of a pool hall near State and Harrison. The weather had driven him inside to watch a floating dice game. He was wishing he had the nerve to kill himself when the front door burst open.

"The cops! Out the side door! Cops out front!"

In the sudden confusion, two men escaped by the side door. One of them was Art Petznick. He says now that was the first and smallest of a series of miracles.

Safe outside, he shuffled south on State Street. A cold rain soaked him to the skin. His head was down and his hair plastered over his eyes. Someone stuck a wet piece of paper in his hand.

"Here ya are, buddy!"

"Huh?" Art raised his head. "Wh-what ya w-want?"

"Come on in and dry out. You can eat and get a good night's sleep on a real bed. This is the Pacific Garden Mission!"

"W-w-w-well. . . ."

"Go on inside! I *have* to stay out here for guys like you. But *you* don't have to drown. Go on in!"

Art did, and miracle number two took place that same night.

"Dad" Taylor was the Mission Superintendent in those days, and he made Jesus Christ "come alive" for Art Petznick. He explained the forgiveness of Christ in a way that made beautiful sense. And Art became another in the long succession of men who have been given new lives in the old Mission prayer room.

From the very beginning, Art meant business with the

Lord. If this thing was real, and he knew it was, then it called for something real on his part, too. Art stayed on at the Mission and attended all the services. Within a few days he knew God was calling him into His service. This was a frightening thought, and he hurried to "Dad" Taylor's office.

"D-dd-dad—h-how d-do you know, wh-wh-when God c-calls you?"

"Why, you just *know*, Art. That is one thing you just— know! And if you turn Him down, He just disturbs you and closes other doors until you say 'yes'."

"M-maybe I'm wrong ab-about it. C-c-could th-that b-bb-be?"

"He doesn't want 'cooked-up' responses, Art. He'll let you know definitely if He wants you. Beyond a shadow of a doubt!"

Art already knew. But he kept hoping he was mistaken. What possible use could God have for a man with a hopeless stammer? Art went through torture every time he stood up to testify at a Mission service. He wanted so much to tell what the Lord had done for him, but his tongue tied itself in knots.

One thing Art *could* do. He went to a Bible school and signed up for classes. A miracle made that possible, too.

He needed two dollars for a registration fee, but was too shy to borrow it from Mr. Taylor. The night before the money was due, a total stranger walked up to him on the street—and handed him two dollars! That made three little miracles.

The fourth happened the next day. He was registering at the school when the man behind the desk looked up and asked a question.

"Mr. Petznick, do you own a Bible?"

"N-no, sir. I b-bb-borrowed one f-from th-the M-m-mission."

"Come this way, please."

He led the way to a private office and handed Art a brand new Scofield Bible.

"Here you are, my friend. The Lord told me to do this!"

So Art had his Bible. But he also had his stammer, and the classes were a real torment. To make matters worse, he discovered he was in love. Her name was Ebba, and she was in several of his classes. When graduation drew near in 1937, he made a tremendous, red-faced, halting effort to tell her how he felt.

It was a horrible failure, as he'd known it would be.

Ebba let him struggle for a minute or two. Then she quietly stopped him.

"You'd better let me say it, Art."

"B-bb-b-but w-wait! I w-want t-tt-to. . . ."

"I know. So let's just save time. I'll answer your question before you ask it, just to prove we're both on the same beam. The answer is 'yes'."

Art says, "You see—how He took me off the hook on that one?"

God had done a great deal for Art Petznick, but the old handicap was still there. Art couldn't say three words without stammering. His Bible studies were completed, he had a head full of sermons, but his rebellious tongue made him helpless.

Then a classmate asked Art to *preach* in a little Polish church. And Art Petznick, the man who couldn't even carry on a conversation, said, "Wh-why, sure"!

Later, he wondered if the years of bad whiskey and canned heat had affected his brain. He went to his room and prayed as he had never prayed before. This was the "agonizing prayer" that rises from only our deepest needs.

As Art begged for help from above, it seemed to him the Lord answered, *"Art, if I could save your soul, I can loosen your tongue. . . ."*

Real peace poured over him, and he opened his Bible and started preparing his sermon. He chose the text in the fifty-third chapter of Isaiah that speaks of Jesus. *"All we like sheep have gone astray; we have turned every one to his own way; and the Lord hath laid on him the iniquity of us all."*

The night he was to preach, Art knew he had a well-prepared sermon. But during the introduction, he thought seriously of running up the aisle and out the door. Instead, a moment later, he found himself standing at the pulpit.

He opened his mouth—and nothing came out. He wanted to thank the friend who had introduced him, but remembered that "th" sounds had always thrown him. Then he remembered that *all* words threw him.

He was so confused that even the text left his mind. He stood staring down at Ebba, his new wife, in the third row. Seconds ticked away and all he could do was say in his mind, over and over again, "Jesus—Jesus—Jesus!"

Again he opened his mouth. Slowly, very slowly at first, words began to flow.

"I've decided—to use as my text this evening—the sixth verse of the fifty-third chapter of Isaiah. . . ."

He was hesitant, but every trace of stammering had vanished. And as Art gained confidence in the reality of the miracle, his sermon flowed more and more smoothly. At times it was actually eloquent.

Ebba was the first person to reach him after the service.

"Art, darling—you were wonderful!"

"But—Ebba, I still don't—believe it."

"You just stood up there and—and *talked*!"

He had a sudden thought.

"Maybe—maybe it was just that once. I only asked for the Lord's help for *tonight*. Maybe I'll start stammering again."

"No, Art. Our Lord doesn't do *anything* in half-way measures. Go on—talk! Talk a blue streak!"

Art Petznick's tongue had been loosened. The speech impediment never returned. But even this didn't make life a soft bed of roses. Christ wants durable followers who can keep going in the tough places. He said as much when He sent Ananias to find Paul with the words, *". . . I will show him how great things he must suffer for my name's sake."*

Art was offered a full-time pastorate in Glenwood, Illinois. The salary was—*three dollars and fifty cents a week.*

He and Ebba prayed all one night about it. It was Ebba who brought the prayer session to a close.

"Now, Lord," she prayed, "We both know you want us to take that pastorate. We've just been shying away from that ridiculous salary. But now we're ready to obey. You promised You'd take care of our needs if we seek You and Your kingdom first. So, Lord—here we go—for three dollars and fifty cents, *plus* all the 'riches in Christ Jesus'."

It was a brave decision, but it still had to be tested. They were actually unpacking their few belongings in Glenwood when a letter arrived. It offered a pastorate in Omaha at $125 a month *plus* a parsonage.

The new offer sounded wonderful. But Ebba said, "Wait a minute, Art. We'd better ask the Lord about this."

So down on their knees they went. And there amid the packing cases and excelsior they knew that God was asking them to stay in Glenwood. They wrote a letter declining the Omaha offer and went back to unpacking.

One of the first problems in their "three-fifty" pastorate had to do with fund raising. Some of the ladies of the church insisted on holding a bazaar in the church basement. To Art, this just didn't seem like God's way. He stood firm in his position that God would provide anything that was in His will. All Art got was argument.

Ebba had her usual answer.

"Down on your knees, honey."

"What?"

"Right now, before I go to the ladies' meeting. You didn't get anywhere with them, so let's ask Him to fix it. Bazaars may not be wrong, but I think they're unnecessary. Let's give the question to God."

Three hours later, Art watched Ebba coming up the walk from the ladies' meeting in a torrential downpour of rain. She was laughing as she closed the door and hung up her raincoat to dry.

"Art, He's done it again! *The fountains of the great deep (were) broken up, and the windows of heaven were opened!*"

"It's a deluge, all right. But what are you so happy about?"

"He's answered another prayer. The bazaar is off!"

"What? How come?"

"'*The waters of the flood were upon the earth,*'—and they left a lake in the church basement. So the ladies very wisely took that as a sign from God that you were right and they were wrong."

The question of bazaars never came up again. Nor did the church close for lack of money. Instead, the congregation outgrew the old building, and within two years had built and paid for a larger one. What's more, the pastor's salary went up to a princely fifteen dollars—every week.

At "recession" prices, Art and Ebba were just able to make ends meet. But when their two children came along, they desperately needed a washing machine. When they had talked it all over Ebba said, "Down on your knees, honey."

"On the subject of a washing machine?"

"Yes—on the subject of a washing machine."

They knew the washer was far beyond their reach, but well within God's.

Several days later Art came home from a round of calls to find a beautiful, brand-new washing machine standing in the kitchen. Neither he nor Ebba had ordered it, so he phoned the store to report a mistaken delivery. The manager assured him it had gone to the right place.

"But, who sent it to us?"

"Sorry. The customer requested that his name be withheld."

It's no wonder that when their family outgrew the tiny house, they asked God for help. But they didn't keep fretting about it. They simply laid the problem before Him, left it with Him, and forgot all about it.

Art says, "If you keep worrying over your needs and snatching your problems back from God, you can tie even His hands."

So, the housing problem was solved, too. An old lady came to the Petznicks with her settled decision.

"I've been a member of this church all my married life, and I haven't long to live. But I *do* have money and a vacant lot. You give the orders, and I'll build a house on that lot to fit your needs. . . . No—don't give me any backtalk! The Lord told me to do this. I'm too old to start disobeying Him now!"

And the house was built.

Art and Ebba have a much bigger church now, in Phoenix, Arizona. But *they're* just the same, and they know their Lord *never* changes. Art makes a very sound observation.

He says, "We have to work as though everything depended upon us, and pray as though everything depended upon—God!"

Cecil Carnes

. . . no leg to stand on

THERE ARE ENDLESS WAYS FOR A MAN TO SLIP DOWN AND down until he hits rock-bottom. But there's only one way up—One Way that's trustworthy and Eternal. Jesus said, *"I am* the way." And there is no other.

Cecil Carnes found his own way down—and then was *found* by the only Way up.

The unique thing about Cecil Carnes is that he never had the slightest intention of being anything else but a success. He had what it took to be outstanding, and that's just what he planned to be.

He was born on a farm near Charleston, Illinois, of a wonderfully easy-going father and a little French pepper-pot of a mother. They often disagreed, usually over one of his father's charming impracticalities. But it takes two to make a quarrel, and Cecil's father never bothered to hold up his end of an argument.

Cecil was a retiring, detached boy who spent a lot of time by himself, dreaming his own big dreams. They all had to do with shining achievements and big accomplishments, and he did his best to carry them out in everyday life. Whatever Cecil did, he always tried to do better than anyone else.

Even farming, much as he hated it, was a challenge. He learned to plow the straightest furrow and handle horses like an expert. In school he made the highest grades and brought home his report cards like trophies. Most of his dreams were not of wealth, but of being admired.

He won all the admiration a boy could want the year he was fourteen, but the price was a high one. His father had gone to town, leaving Cecil to disk a field with a four-horse hitch.

Something startled the horses. Skillful as the boy was, he lost control. The runaways broke off across the field and Cecil was thrown down. One of the shining, knife-like disks passed over his ankle. A neighbor in the next field saw the accident and came running.

"Cecil! Are you hurt, boy? Are you. . . ." He saw the boy's leg and gasped.

"Oh—son!"

"My—my foot! It hurts *lots,* Mr. Hallec!"

Hallec knelt at Cecil's side.

"I—I reckon it does hurt, son." He hesitated and then told the truth.

"Your foot's layin' thirty feet away—over there by the fence."

"Huh?" Cecil struggled to see. "My foot's—cut off?"

"Mebbe I shouldn't have told you, boy."

"No—it's all right." Cecil had a vision of courage to live up to. "I'd have missed it—anyway."

He raised himself on an elbow and looked at the hemorrhaging stump.

"Mr. Hallec—!"

"Yes, son. We'll have to git you to a doctor right away!"

"Sure, Mr. Hallec—but first we've got to stop the bleedin'. Take the lace outa your shoe—and tie it tight—around my ankle."

"Why, yeah—sure, Cecil—sure."

The farmer fumbled with his boot-lace while Cecil told him what to do.

"I learned that—in school, Mr. Hallec. You see, you have to stop the bleedin'—right away. They call it—applying a tourniquet."

The newspapers made quite a thing of it. They wrote about Cecil's courage and the calm way he took charge of the first-aid treatment. Later, when an amputation had to be done just below the knee, they ran the story all over again with the new developments.

Cecil had all the admiration he needed. It helped, somehow, to make up for the accident and the loss of his leg.

A couple of years later he went on to the University with hopes of becoming a history teacher or a chemist. But when it was time to go back for the sophomore year, his schooling was interrupted. His father broke the news in the fumbling way that was so annoying to Cecil's mother.

"Cecil, your mother and I hate to tell you this, but—ah—but. . . ."

"Get to the point, Hez!" The hemming and hawing was too much for her peppery nature.

"Well, Tinny—don't rush me, now. I keep thinkin' there must be *some* way to work things out."

"No, there isn't! Cecil, there's no possible way you can go back to the University this year, and we might as well all just face up to it."

"I can't go back at all?"

"Not without money. And your father has squandered it all on 'improvements' we didn't need."

Hez Carnes shouldered the blame patiently.

"I *meant* to do the right thing, Cecil. Guess I must have been awful wrong, though. Same as always when it comes to money. I'm sorry, son."

They really did need Cecil's help, and he put in ten solid years on the farm. Each one was pure agony. His brothers left home and followed careers of their own, but Cecil stuck to the place and helped his parents. He wasn't even consciously resentful. Just heart-broken.

It was some relief just to get off the farm when they moved to the town of Mattoon. Cecil found a job of his own, while his parents started an advertising and distributing business. Their operations expanded, and after a few years they asked Cecil to join them on a full-time basis.

The money was good, but the business was really his mother's. Though he did well, the sense of personal accomplishment was lacking. Years were slipping away, and Cecil felt he was getting nowhere. He wondered more and more if he'd ever break loose from his parents and make a name for himself.

Yet when they died, within two years of each other, Cecil felt at loose ends. He'd been chained so long he found freedom uncomfortable. To fill the emptiness he began drinking, not much at first but more and more as time went on. He was still ambitious, and never drank enough in those days to hurt him in a business way.

When a job was offered in a large hotel, Cecil took it.· Hard work paid off and he was promoted to Assistant General Manager. He seemed to have a real bent for hotel work. Bit by bit the owner turned over nearly all the responsibilities to him.

Carnes worked as assistant, and then as General Manager, for more than two years. When he quit, he wasn't really sure of the reason. He just felt—dissatisfied and restless.

In Minneapolis he took a job representing an artificial limb manufacturer. Again the money was good. And again, no satisfaction. His drinking was on the increase.

He moved to Chicago and found a job with a glass company. By gritting his teeth and drinking just a little more all the time, he managed to stick that one out for more than four years.

Misery was becoming a habit with Cecil. He found company in a Czech plumber named John, who was hugging the misery of having lost his wife. They spent most of their weekends at John's house, drinking and watching Class B action pictures on television. Sometimes, drunk as they were, even Cecil and John found the entertainment too poor.

"Let's turn this thing off, Cecil."

"Sure, I saw that picture twice before already."

John reached for the switch and emptied the flickering screen.

"You gonna quit your job at the glass factory?"

"Yeah, John. They don't know it, but I've already quit. Too long, John. Four and a half years too long."

"You get along good."

"Sure—so what?"

"Here, Cecil. Hold out your glass."

"Okay. Hey, John—we gotta call up for some more whiskey pretty soon."

"Yeah. I'm gettin' so I need a lot of it. Thank God for whiskey!"

"That's very funny, John. 'Thank God for whiskey'."

"I don't think much of God. Do you, Cecil?"

"God? I'm not interested in Him, and He's prob'ly not interested in me."

"Me, I don't like God!"

"You got reasons, John. Good reasons."

"Plenty good reasons. If my Elsie hadn't of died, I wouldn't be a no-good drunken bum. Three years now she's gone. God took her away, and still I cry myself to sleep."

"You don't know how lucky you are. You got a *reason* to hate God, John. But me, I've got nothin'—not even a leg to stand on."

Cecil chuckled at his own joke. John was too occupied with his troubles to catch it at once. Then he saw the point and began laughing too.

"You made a good joke, Cecil. Listen, you got a leg to stand on. You got a fine wooden leg to stand on!"

John wiped his eyes and reached for the telephone. It was time to call the liquor store.

In Chicago, Cecil lived with a friendly couple who owned a restaurant and had a big apartment upstairs in the same building. They were fond of Cecil, and his drinking worried them more and more. When his condition grew so bad he was unable to hold a job, he couldn't bear to face the warm-hearted Domenicos any longer. He moved out and drifted from one cheap hotel to another, living on his savings.

The money held out seven months. Then, broke and in pitiful condition, he turned up at his old friends' restaurant. Mrs. Domenico saw him come in the door and helped him to a table.

"Cecil Carnes, are you trying to drink dry every tavern in Chicago?"

He stumbled, and she caught him just in time.

"Here, Cecil. Sit down before you hurt yourself!"

Cecil rummaged through his pockets for money.

"I got—money—to pay for a cup of coffee. You don't have to worry, Mrs. Domenico. I got money—look."

He came up with three dimes.

"See—I told you. Thirty cents—for a cup of coffee. Whatsa matter? Isn' thirty cents enough?"

"I no want t'ree dimes! You sit still and I make a good hot breakfast. Then you go upstairs and sleep."

The Domenicos offered him a job on condition that he stay sober. He promised, stuck it out for several months, then began nipping again. When Mrs. Domenico lectured him, he felt picked on—so he just quit.

His second night on the town, Cecil was jack-rolled and left penniless. He drifted to Kokomo and stayed with a half-sister. That didn't work out. From there he moved on to his old home town of Mattoon where he had other relatives. That didn't work out, either. The relatives bought him a railroad ticket and gave him a little money.

Now, back in Chicago, he wandered up Canal Street to the Northwestern Station. Cecil was sober, but he was sick and scared. He just plain didn't know where to go or what to do next. That's how he happened to approach a total stranger with a pitiful question.

"S'cuse me, mister."

"If you want money—no!"

"I know I look pretty bad, mister. But I don't want money. I've got two dollars."

"Well, then. . . ."

"It's—well, I'm afraid I'll get picked up if I keep on walkin' around the streets. I can't go in a saloon, because if I get started I'll drink up the two dollars. Mister, I've never—I mean, I've always tried to. . . ."

"Get to the point."

"All right—where can I go to keep out of jail?"

"Well now, let me think." The man began to be genuinely concerned. "Try the Pacific Garden Mission."

"Mission?"

"Yeah, it's over on State Street just south of Harrison."

"What kind of a Mission?"

"Well, they've got free food—and beds—and the cops won't bother you."

"Yeah, but is it—a religious layout?"

"Religious? Sure, but you look like a little religion wouldn't hurt you."

Walking across town, Cecil began to think the man might be right. Maybe a little religion wouldn't hurt him. He found the Mission and got the free bed and food. But the service in the chapel left him unmoved.

One person impressed him. It was a dark, handsome young man with a *peaceful* face. He shook Cecil's hand and said, "God loves you, buddy," but Cecil changed the subject. He didn't want this religion business to get out of hand.

In the morning he picked up his one small suitcase and walked out. Except for the free meal and a night's sleep, he was in the same situation he'd been in the day before. The two dollars were still in his pocket, and he still didn't know what to do or where to go.

Cecil wandered toward the lake and sat in the park. Then, for reasons he couldn't really figure out, he headed back toward the Mission. There's a bar across the street from the Old Lighthouse. Cecil went in there and sat down. Three big drinks and a package of cigarettes put a deep dent in his two dollars, so he went outside again and stared across at the Mission door. As he watched, the peaceful-looking young man came out and stood on the sidewalk enjoying the sunshine.

A wild impulse sent Cecil running across the street, as fast as he could go on his wooden leg. He dodged a taxicab and a big truck, ran around the back of a streetcar, and reached the safety of the curb. He tugged at the young man's coat sleeve, and the thing he said was even wilder than his actions.

"Listen—can you save me?"

The young man looked startled.

"No, sir—I can't. But I know Someone Who can."

"Yeah—who?"

"Do you—want to be saved?"

"Look, I'm not even real sure what it means—but I want to be different from the way I am. Listen, will you help me find God?"

That is a question no one needs to ask more than once at Pacific Garden Mission.

In the prayer room, the young man tried to make it clear to Cecil that no one needs to look for God, because He is looking for us through Jesus Christ.

When he fell on his knees to pray, Cecil didn't know one word of Scripture. He didn't understand a shred of doctrine. But the thing he knew beyond all doubt was that he had made a horrible mess of his life, and that he didn't have the power to make it right. So when he had poured out his load of sins and his guilt and fears, he prayed a prayer as simple as the publican's.

"Lord, give me a new life. I can't run my life—stands to reason I can't run it. How could I? I'm not God!"

Right there he stated a truth so simple that it takes some a lifetime to see it. Cecil Carnes still can't run his own life, and he knows he'll never be able to. But that doesn't bother him at all.

Because Cecil Carnes belongs to Christ. And Christ is God.